D1572018

# An Unspeakable Betrayal

# AN UNSPEAKABLE BETRAYAL

## Selected Writings of Luis Buñuel

With a Foreword by
Jean-Claude Carrière

and a New Afterword by
Juan Luis Buñuel
and Rafael Buñuel

Translated from the Spanish
and French by Garrett White

University of California Press
Berkeley  Los Angeles  London

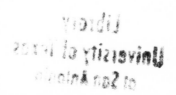

Originally published in French as *Le Christ à cran d'arrêt: oeuvres littéraires*, © 1995 Luis Buñuel Estate c/o Librairie Plon, Paris. All texts have been newly translated from the original languages for this edition.

The translation of "Why I Don't Wear a Watch" appeared, in a slightly different version, in *Grand Street* 59 (winter 1997): 18–22.

The photo of Buñuel in *Un Chien andalou* (p. ii) is used courtesy Luis Buñuel Estate.

University of California Press
Berkeley and Los Angeles, California

University of California Press, Ltd.
London, England

© 2000 by The Regents of the University of California

Library of Congress Cataloging-in-Publication Data

Buñuel, Luis, 1900–
    [Christ à cran d'arrêt. English]
    An unspeakable betrayal : selected writings of Luis Buñuel / with a foreword by Jean-Claude Carrière ; and a new afterword by Juan Luis Buñuel and Rafael Buñuel ; translated from the Spanish and French by Garrett White.
      p.  cm.
    ISBN 0-520-20840-4 (paper : alk. paper)
    I. White, Garrett.  II. Title.
PQ2603.U55C4713 2000
868'.6409—dc21                     99-43048
                                     CIP

Manufactured in the United States of America

08  07  06  05  04  03  02  01  00  99
10  9  8  7  6  5  4  3  2  1

The paper used in this publication meets the minimum requirements of ANSI/NISO Z39.48-1992 (R 1997) (*Permanence of Paper*). ♾

# Contents

## On Cinema

## Buñuel on Buñuel

## Autobiographical Writings

# Acknowledgments

The publisher wishes to thank Professor Julie Jones for her generous assistance with this project.

For their help in the completion of the translation, the translator would like to thank Eulogio Guzmán, Karen Hansgen, and Antonio Mendoza. Special thanks to Edward Dimendberg, formerly of the University of California Press, and above all to UC Press editor Rose Vekony, whose sensitive reading of the manuscript improved it immeasurably.

# Foreword

Jean-Claude Carrière

Buñuel didn't like his writing—his *letra*, to use the Spanish word. He was loath to write a letter by hand, preferring to tap out his correspondence with two fingers at the typewriter.

But did he like *to write?* I think not. He was a man of silence, of meditation. While at work on a screenplay, he found endless pleasure in the manifold, disconcerting games of the imagination. He considered those the best moments of his life. He loved to laugh, play, improvise, tell stories—sometimes subtle variations of the same story several times a day. The clumsiness of filming, which he accepted as a necessary chore (to be done with as quickly as possible), bored him a bit. Cinema, he would say, is like a dresser who suddenly presents you with two pairs of shoes and asks: which ones for the ballroom scene? And there has to be a response. The director can never grant himself the luxury of answering "I don't know" or "I could care less."

And writing? Solitary work at a desk? Buñuel very rarely engaged in it. Nor does a writer ever figure among the characters in his films. He would sometimes envy the guarded solitude of painters, and the physicality of their occupation, but never that of writers. With perhaps one or two exceptions, he didn't write his own screenplays. That task always fell to his scriptwriter (which I was for eighteen years), who by night was charged with giving form to notes—frequently disordered, if not incoherent—taken during daytime improvisations. On the following morning, we would read over these drafts together, often throwing them out, at other times correcting them, and so on.

He kept writing at a distance. The film was already moving and talking in his head. Committing it to paper, which tends to freeze things, seemed to him difficult, almost dangerous, and in any case risky.

Nevertheless, in his youth he was tempted to write, and indeed he did write, as we shall see: poems, articles, film projects. He had things to say—I think everyone agrees on that. He also had, as has often been said, a natural predisposition toward surrealism, the mark of which can be seen very clearly in these pages. He wrote (with Dalí) and filmed *Un Chien andalou* before he was even aware of the group's activities in Paris.

Later, after he had become a filmmaker, he made several forays into what we might call "assisted writing," working with a collaborator just as he would on a script. Specifically, I wrote the piece found in this book under the title *Medieval Memories of Lower Aragón* not exactly under his dictation, but after long conversations, of which I made precise notes. This text would later appear in *My Last Sigh*, the only book to come out under Buñuel's name in his lifetime, which I wrote. But I wrote it with him, in Mexico, conferring with him for three hours a day and then daring to write, "I, Buñuel . . ." Eighteen years of working side by side with him gave me license to do so. And in any event, he reread everything, rejecting one or two sentences (though rarely) and changing a word here and there.

He was quite well read, indeed very properly cultured. Along with sports, reading was the great passion of his youth. In particular, he loved then, and throughout his life, the French novelists of the late nineteenth century—Huysmans, Octave Mirbeau, Pierre Louÿs—writers who in Spain in the years 1915–20 still smacked somewhat of heresy. He loved the Spaniard Pérez Galdós and the picaresque novel (above all *Lazarillo de Tormes*), the romantic poet Bécquer, and M. G. Lewis's *The Monk*. His knowledge of the Russian novelists, especially Dostoevsky, surprised André Gide when they met in Paris. Among the surrealist writers, he ranked Benjamin Péret above all others; for him Péret was the most innocent, the most natural, the freshest. "Surrealism flowed from his lips," he often said.

But he was, I believe, a born filmmaker. If he had poetic aspirations as a young man, they abandoned him the moment he met García Lorca at the students' residence hall in Madrid. If he didn't care much for his friend's theater, he more than made up for it with his love of García Lorca's poetry. He went so far as to recopy by hand a poem García Lorca had written for him in pencil that had begun to fade. From time to time, even very much later, he would suddenly speak a few lines from the *Romancero* that had come to him unexpectedly.

He said that García Lorca, without any doubt, had opened the doors to another world for him, an expanding world. When he went to Paris at twenty-five, the discovery of Russian and German films (above all those of Fritz Lang and Murnau) showed him his true path. That was what he was born for: that explosion on a white screen.

His literary reticence (we might almost call it shyness) makes the texts we are about to read—as if rescued from the deep—that much more precious. They are the fragments of a writer who might have been, a lost writer, a phantom writer hidden behind an immense filmmaker. But the man is there, for those who know him well, present in every word—sarcastic and sentimental, brutal and modest.

It seems that he watched the world through words as through a lens. No doubt many will be surprised to find here a lecture on puppet shows and astonishing commentaries on the film version of *Camille* or on Adolphe Menjou's mustache. All of Buñuel is here, or nearly: his somber irony, his shocking taste for paradox, his secret attraction to melodrama. We also get a sense of his fascination for cinema, something he never expressly acknowledged. Indeed, sometimes he despised his own work, even detested the art in general, and publicly declared that he would willingly burn the negatives of all of his films. Occasionally, when passing by the tawdry façades of certain movie theaters along the Gran Vía in Madrid, he would fly into a rage and say that he felt ashamed.

Nevertheless, at one point in an essay in this book he speaks of cinema as "an almost perfect language of signs." This language can be turned into a weapon for subverting reality, for bursting convention and assassinating idleness, "a marvelous and dangerous weapon when handled by a free spirit." This book takes us in search of those signs, of that language of invention.

*From the French.*

# SURREALIST WRITINGS

# An Unspeakable Betrayal

For a whole year I had been laboring on *my* work, *my* great work. I was spending five, six, ten hours of every day on this crowning achievement, and already the world's finest literary magazines were fighting to get it. The furniture, the parquet floor, the books in my room were all delighted to see me toiling at this work of genius. As soon as I sat down, the table, the bookcase, and the bed crowded around me, chirping contentedly. The bookcase in particular, which would draw closer, on tiptoes, and arch its ribs of books expectantly. A spider at work on a large house under construction in a corner always slid down a scaffold pulley and nodded in assent with its legs.

My only enemy, goading and quarrelsome, was the wind. Almost every night, before entering my room, I left him whistling cheerfully, entwined by the power lines in the street or cavorting with the papers that grazed on the stone pavement. But scarcely had I finished undressing, as the obliging easy chair shook the dust from itself, opening its cordial arms to receive me, when he began to throw violent punches at the window's spine, looking for an opportunity to sneak in or trying to open it by force; but my window crossed its two sinewy, solitary fingers tightly and scoffed at the wind. The wind, to avenge himself, badgered the walls with savage impetuousness, whistling loudly and hurling handfuls of dust and pebbles against the glass. But I, despite everything, retained my composure and kept working.

Finally, one night he promised that if I would let him in to admire my work, he would never bother me again; on the contrary, he would bring me all kinds of perfumes and music and coo softly to *my* great work.

Tempted by the offer, and furthermore, I must confess, by a slight tinge of legitimate pride in having so important a figure take an interest in my work, I was inclined to consent. The wind, howling with delight, uprooted two trees, spun a few houses forty-five degrees, and swung all the bells of the city in triumphal peals. Not content with this, he showed off as a magician. He turned three priests sneaking down the street into as many inverted umbrellas; he made Himalayas of streets and houses enveloped in his clouds; and, at his conjuring, cafe tables sprouted rags, documents, straws, and other objects from the Great Costume Jewelry Store of the Garbage Dump.

At last, considering how eager he was to please me, I decided to let him in and opened the window.

The grotesque wind rushed headlong over the sills and sniffed restlessly at everything. Where he caused real terror was in the basket of papers; they were resting peacefully there, but upon perceiving the presence of the monster, they caprioled madly one on top of the other, swirling about and fleeing in all directions before taking shelter in the tub and beneath the wardrobe, for the wind is paper's cat.

Frankly, I was angered at his impropriety and the lack of interest he had shown in perusing *my* work, for which I admonished him severely. Then, feigning close attention, he reviewed the thousands of pages, shuffling them as loudly as a conjurer does a deck of cards; suddenly, with a single slap, he threw them into space through the dumbfounded window, which had opened its big mouth in amazement, and set out after them.

I was crushed, dazed, torn apart forever, like a book from its cover. He had carried off *my* work, *my* definitive work, which was flying, transformed into seagulls, across the horizon.

I swore to avenge myself without delay. I soon found a way to do it. When I saw him asleep on the roof, where the chimneys were also yawning, lulled by his snoring, I installed a different window that barely fit and would occasionally come off its hinge. And he fell into the trap.

As usual, upon waking he threw himself against the window, but this time he found himself captured, vanquished, defeated by the cracks.

For years now he has been wailing mournfully and pleading for his freedom. Unyielding, I will keep him there, handcuffed to the interstices of the window, which is always closed and always sure of itself. *I'm not one to play games with.*

*From the Spanish. Published in* Ultra *(Madrid), February 1, 1922.*

# Orchestration

for Adolfo Salazar

*Violins*

Pretentious young ladies of the orchestra, insufferable and pedantic. Jagged mountains of sound.

*Violas*

Violins that have just entered menopause. These spinsters still retain their half-tone voices.

*Violoncello*

Murmurs of sea and woods. Serenity. Deep eyes. They have the conviction and the grandeur of Jesus' sermons in the desert.

*Contrabass*

Diplodocus of instruments. Oh, the day they decide to let loose their great bellowing, driving away the terrified spectators! For now, we see them oscillate and growl with contentment as the contrabassists tickle their stomachs.

*Piccolo*

Anthill of sound.

*Flute*

The flute is the most nostalgic instrument. That she who in the hands of Pan was the thrilling voice of meadow and forest should now find herself in the hands of a fat, bald fellow . . . ! But even so, she remains the Princess of instruments.

*Clarinet*

A hypertrophied flute. Now and then, poor thing, he sounds all right.

*Oboe*

Bleating become wood. Its waves, profound lyrical mysteries. The oboe was Verlaine's twin brother.

*Tenor Oboe*

The mature, experienced oboe. Well traveled. Its exquisite temperament has become more serious, more inspired. If the oboe is fifteen years old, the tenor oboe is thirty.

*Bassoon*

Bassoonists are the fakirs of the orchestra. Now and then, they watch the terrible reptile they hold in their hands, as it shows them its forked tongue. Once they've hypnotized it, they lay it in their arms and become ecstatic.

*Contrabassoon*

The bassoon of the Tertiary Period.

*Xylophone*

A child's game. Water of wood. Princesses knitting in the garden, moonbeams.

*Trumpet with Mute*

Clown of the orchestra. Contortion, pirouette. Grimaces.

*French Horns*

Climbing toward a summit. Sunrise. Annunciation. Oh, the day they unfurl like a streamer!

*Trombones*

A slightly German temperament. Prophetic voice. Succentors in an ancient cathedral with ivy and a rusty weather vane.

*Tuba*

Legendary dragon. The other instruments tremble with fear at its boom-
ing, subterranean voice and wonder when the prince in burnished armor
will come to deliver them.

*Cymbals*

Light shattered into fragments.

*Triangle*

A silver streetcar through the orchestra.

*Drum*

Little toy thunder. "Somewhat" menacing.

*Bass Drum*

Obfuscation. Coarseness. Boom. Boom. Boom.

*Timpani*

Skins filled with olives.

*From the Spanish. Published in* Horizonte *(Madrid), no. 2, November 30, 1922.*

# Suburbs: Motifs

Suburbs, outskirts, the last houses of the city. It is to this absurd conglomeration of earthen walls, heaps of dirt, hovels, withered scraps of countryside, etc., that the following motifs refer.

These aren't the great suburbs of a London: tough, sordid, but full of working-class activity. Rather, they are those of the small provincial capital, inhabited by poor and indolent people, rag-and-bone folks at most.

These suburbs have the anodyne, expressive complexity of an attic. They're like a room into which the city tosses all its worn-out things. Everything moth-eaten or useless can be found there.

In this absurd aesthetic so characteristic of the suburb, everything is forsaken, symbolized by the objects that appear before us: the empty tin can, the hungry dog, the eviscerated mouse, or the twisted, dust-covered gaslight.

Its entire psychological and material perspective—hostile and sad— is relegated to the depths of our spirits. The soul of the suburb strangles any glimmer of life or movement the place might have. In the aquarelle that we immediately paint with the palette of our feelings, we can use only one color: gray.

All the noises and gratings that roar in the great mouth of the city become obsessive there, set into the monotony that smears the suburban atmosphere. Joy hangs in tatters from the eaves, barely stirred by the breeze of small voices, those of the children who sift through the heaps, to whom no one ever tells stories.

Here and there, our eyes—which survey the suburbs with the selfish "God forgive, brother" of fallen things—are offended by a "Tavern" sign, spelled out in decrepit letters, sick to the marrow, for here the word has even lost the strong and vibrant quality that, like wine, it boasts of elsewhere. From the balconies, set out like rags to dry, hang the innumerable crimes pointed out again and again in the streets by the blind man with his cane and placard.

We see from time to time, taking shelter behind the walls of some would-be corral, the heaps of dirt adulterated with the hundred indistinct, useless objects—because a hundred hands have already removed what was useful in them—that bury our imagination as if in a ditch. Those corrals suffer from nostalgia for the sound of bleating, and on the backs of their ocher walls there are dirty, forgotten jewels of verbena.

In the subjective view of the suburb at dusk, everything becomes more heartrendingly inert. Our souls are whipped gloomily by a rag hung from an electric cable or the echoless shouts that ply the air like bats. In the distance, the dim gaslight winks its failing eye, and the frayed shadows take refuge in the doorjambs, spreading out their silent hands as if begging for something.

The interminable yawn of the suburb and its reddened, faded eyes are always the terrible curse of the city. Even when the day dances happily across the nearby rooftops, it is immediately caught in the snare of the suburb's perennial sadness, which paints a black stroke across the boisterous joy of the metropolis. These lethargic districts belong to the camp of the hopeless, the fatal. Their emotion of dead trees. The inhabitants have been victims of the rabid bite of the suburb's soul. The only cure for this suburbophobia is a preventive injection of a few sacks of gold.

Among the cortège of words, there is Suburb, dressed in rags, stained with grease, and on its face the stigma of the tramp who sleeps in the doorways of houses.

*From the Spanish. Published in* Horizonte, *no. 4 (Madrid), January 1923.*

## Unnoticed Tragedies as Themes for a Totally New Theater

Of all literary genres, the theater is certainly the least exploited. From primitive times to the present, it has fundamentally undergone little or no variation.

Ibsen first, then Wedekind were those chosen to mark out a new orientation in this art, still in its long-lived infancy. And Maeterlinck and Apollinaire? Did they do anything other than revise the old structural composition, tackling eternal yet outdated themes in a new way?

The aesthetic problem before us is to construct, to introduce "new" and "original" themes that have not been treated by any universal dramaturgy. Even if the *Chauve-Souris* revue succeeded in masterfully molding the range of emotions that the theater tends to awaken, nevertheless, its means of expression were, if not old, then at least lacking interests of continuity. How do we fuse this interest with the novelty of the subject?

Surely the inanimate can provide us with abundant themes. It's true that some lifeless object is often made to speak, but usually as if it were a human being or with lyricisms that surpass the greatest of poets. The lyrical and philosophical expression is there, but not the psychological expression innate to them—this tremendous and complex psychology still so little explored.

Ultimately, the drama, comedy, or what have you about the customs and passions of these strange characters, should it fail to impress a human audience, could instead bring tears, laughter, or thrills to the other audience of chairs, kitchen utensils, etc., etc.

But what is certain is that passions do exist in the world of the abiotic.

A few years ago I bought a small chamois cloth, because it seemed nice to me in the shop window where it resided. I used to hang it on a nail by my window, and there it went on existing tranquilly. When I entered my room, it gleefully moved its little angular arms and didn't stop signaling me until I took it in my hands. It clung to them tenderly, communicating its sweet warmth with affection that can only be compared to that of a mother caressing her child. Its rag tongue would tell me things that were inexplicable to me, only a human being, after all. If before I began to clean my glasses I didn't stroke its smooth, diminutive head of hair, it would wrap itself around my fingers and not let go until it received the desired caress. In the end both he and I became truly fond of each other. To see him smile through his creases on sunny days, or cry, wrinkled and battered, when it rained!

Then one day I noticed that he wasn't in his place. I remembered his clever trick in the past of hiding behind the furniture. When I couldn't find him, I knew that something terrible had happened.

I spent three or four months in a sadness that could only be explained by the disappearance of my little friend. But one day as I was heading toward the outskirts of town, I was stupefied by the sight of a dreadful tableau. A strong wind made the road posts bellow in pain, and armies of clouds in purple uniforms traversed the sky sowing extermination. In the midst of this scene, dangling from a telegraph wire, lay my unforgettable rag, dead. He was enveloped in an otherworldly sorrow, his heartbreaking tatters moving in the wind, pecked dispassionately by rain and wind. Even now it moves me just to think about it.

This sad event illustrates the reciprocal tenderness that the inanimate sometimes offers us.

And this deep affection that we have for our pipe, teapot, cane, or necktie—isn't that perhaps the fitting response to their favors?

I know of a pipe that was picked up from a friend's table by a hard-hearted man, who abducted it without compassion. Well then, when the vile abductor went to light it, it singed his nose. That infuriated pipe spewed burning ash from its only eye.

Another time, one of those plump earthen jugs, with a sharp beak, choked up and refused to give me its cooling streams if every day I didn't scatter a few crumbs on the floor, which it gobbled up, making little hops and leaning over with comical clumsiness.

For a theater of the macabre, à la *Edgar Poe*, the dramatist of the new generation can find inspiration in the attics of houses, and leave behind those shop-worn cemeteries. In attics, "top-floor municipal cemeteries," one can find old chests of drawers, their stomachs distended by the final illness, limping on their feet during midnight sabbats. Birdcages lacking all sense of proportion. Grotesque luggage trunks, still gripped with the terror inspired by death. This entire funerary procession standing honor guard over the one who was once a brazier, still encased in the iron armor in which it was interred. Finally, there is the macabre smell of dead crockery so common in attics.

I happened to be reading the paper when suddenly I heard a sharp groan from the clothes rack. My brilliant pajamas, only recently purchased, had just committed suicide by leaping to the floor. My shock was complete when I realized that what I had been reading about was an enormous fire at the Great House of Fabrics, the store where I had purchased them. The flames, bent on plunder, had totally destroyed it. Had the pajamas perhaps read about the death of their brethren, or sensed it? I don't know; the fact is, the affective is a quality of the inanimate.

*From the Spanish. Published in* Alfar *(La Coruña), no. 26, February 1923.*

# Why I Don't Wear a Watch

I was writing a letter of no importance, so what I am about to relate was not a suggestion produced by an altered state of consciousness, nor could it have been a dream, since a few moments earlier I had been hunting down an impertinent fly that kept bothering me by speaking into my ear—like those old deaf people who whisper, low and laboriously, insufferable things—and on the day after my adventure I found its corpse in a coffin formed by the lid of the inkwell.

So there I was, writing. Suddenly I heard nearby a ticktock louder than the others, as if its whole point were to get my attention; to my profound amazement, I found myself face to face with a being stranger than any the imagination could devise.

It had two legs, one a pencil and the other a pen; its body took the shape of a rusty steel rod, and its head was nothing more than a gilded brass disk, with an uneven mustache in the form of two arrows and two minuscule crowns for eyes, like the kind used to wind wristwatches. Everything about him demonstrated a truly intolerable air of affectation and vanity.

Astonished, but no less offended, I questioned him: "Would you mind telling me why you have entered my room without having had the decency to knock?"

The extravagant little fellow, unfazed by my gruffness, replied very casually: "You've been going around with me since the day you were born, Mr. Muckamuck, and until now you've never deigned to ask me such questions."

Irritated by his contemptuous tone, I said, "Mind your tongue, and don't call me Mr. Muckamuck, because I have other, more honorific titles"—and to prove it I was about to take from my desk the documents conferring them.

"Calm down, young man," he told me. "I am older than you could possibly dream, and my age gives me the right to use this authoritarian tone."

"Well, then, who are you?"

"I am Time."

An Oh! of stupefaction drew a perfect circle on my mouth. But he hastened to continue: "Don't be frightened; after all, I only materialized in this form out of pure sympathy for you. More important, I wish to make revelations that perhaps might interest you."

At that, he settled comfortably onto a cushion. In further astonishment, I saw the alarm clock and the clock on the wall leave their places and, wagging their tails, come over to lick his feet. There could no longer be any doubt that this was indeed Time himself to whom I was talking. Now I will transcribe his story in its entirety.

Here is what he said: "My friend, tonight I have undertaken a bold gesture. I myself have annulled several hours of Eternity.

"No one but you will know that nothing will age while I am here, and all that exists will have disappeared. But I am going to speak to you about my life. My whole life story can be divided into two periods: before the invention of clocks, and from then until now. My first era glided along in joyful frolicking with my brother Space everywhere we ruled in the Universe. We had a great time, upon my soul!, and only one tiny cloud ruffled our existence. It was something of a gastronomic nature. Can you believe there wasn't a single kitchen, not one restaurant, not even a pasture? A complete lack of food is what drove me to devour my children as soon as they were born. Later I saw myself portrayed as a monstrous and ferocious old man, turned theophagous through egotism and evil instincts. But I solemnly swear"—as he said this, his pendulum swung gracefully across his stomach—"that these so-called crimes were committed only to satisfy my appetite. On the other hand, eating one's children belongs to a code of ethics that was very fashionable some five or six thousand years ago."

He said "five or six thousand years" the way you or I would say "three or four days."

"But my friend, ever since the first clock appeared"—and his rather erect and martial mustache now marked 7 and 25—"there hasn't been a moment's rest for me. I must multiply myself, raise myself to the $n^{th}$ power to be able to run every clock in existence. You might have noticed that I can't always keep up with so much work, and when that happens my enemies are in the habit of falling silent. The agitation has been excessive for at least a few centuries, despite which you will sometimes hear and even read, 'Time passed tranquilly . . .' 'Time quietly promised . . .' But believe me, those are nothing more than lies and foolishness, to which you should pay no attention."

At this point, a slight throat irritation struck him, and he coughed 8:00. Scarcely able to ticktock, amidst the jubilant barking of my two clocks, which were also chiming 8:00, he went on: "I see here you have a portrait of that half-wit Einstein. Experience has armored me against insults, but the offense of relativity has grieved me above all others. As if the falsehoods raised against me weren't enough, it turns out I'm now the subject of everyone's gossip, thanks to this depraved person."

Suddenly his body began to lengthen inordinately. I swung around anxiously in my chair upon seeing a new prodigy in that phantasmagorical night. Time had stretched out too far.

"Don't worry," he told me, already completely calm, "in a moment I'll finish and be gone. But I'm not leaving without first helping you in whatever way possible. Of course, when old age comes to grab you in his trembling claws, I'll be there to stop him and keep you eternally young."

"Thanks, but no thanks," I replied quickly, "I want my time to come like everyone else's."

"You're a sensible man," he answered. "Since you refuse this, I will count you among my beloved children, and favor you as I do them."

"Then I'd like to know who my brothers will be."

"For God's sake! Well, your brothers will be watch thieves and swindlers, because they do much to lighten my load by making off with those little instruments that are the most annoying to me, since they are so numerous. Lazy people are also my children, for they use me in moderation. My children are—"

"Don't go on," I said abruptly. "You want to throw me in with swindlers, with idlers? No way will I accept your favors."

"You're an inexperienced young man, far too ingenuous. Open your eyes to the fact that they are the ones who have lived best, along with the many others I was about to cite. If you were an artist, you would love, for example, just a few hours of tedium, my favorite son."

"I'm beginning to see that your most beloved children are the traits most discredited among men. You're proving to be a vagrant, unscrupulous, selfish being."

Time was threatening to storm. His minute and hour hands were growing angry. He struck 8:30 in such a menacing way that I began to feel genuine fear.

"Enough, young man. Since you disdain my favors, you will suffer my disfavor. In the meantime, within two days you will be left without clocks." Having said this, he suddenly disappeared.

And his curse was fulfilled, for not two days after my adventure, I found myself without a dime and had to pawn my two dear clocks.

What's more, I fell prey to a constant obsession. Every clock I ran into glared at me threateningly; their hands bristled with wrath. Others, when I wanted to know what time it was, would spin disconcertingly, as if to mock me.

So I bought myself an hourglass and placed it on the table. But then the vengefulness of Time was bloodier still. I don't know what he did with it, but the fact is, its slender waist, a waist as thin as a needle, widened little by little until it allowed the sand to pass in thick streams.

Then I came to detest that poor, plump hourglass, which after all was not to blame for its disgrace, and one day I threw it out the window, like those intolerant masters of the house who cast out a maid who slips up.

Since then, I have resigned myself to getting by without a watch, which has made me lose some very good friends when I fail to show up at our meetings.

*From the Spanish. Published in* Alfar *(La Coruña), no. 29, May 1923.*

# Theorem

If from a point outside of a straight line we draw a parallel line, we will obtain a sunny autumn afternoon.

In fact:

The sky, all blue eyes, reflects the fishless dream of ponds, and these in turn tepidly bathe the laziness of the afternoon.

The blind trees pass by in a slow procession, and in their highest branches a straggling leaf chirps gold.

The streets want to leave en masse for a stroll in the country, but so slowly that the travelers soon leave them behind, trembling in the sun.

Yellowish fields climb hills and bluffs and stretch out there, legs spread, waiting for the night. Only a few poplars, always restless, telegraph a Morse code of leaves.

Measured breathing of the afternoon, and all things beating to its rhythm.

Me, I carry in the palm of my hand my cane without leaves.

A breast sleeps purring in the sun.

All the windows have eyelashes like women.

The church tower, like a forefinger, points to the last tiny white cloud.

Silence after a hum, then Christ passes by selling voices.

The swallows kiss the beak of seven o'clock.

A volley of weathercocks in the air.

The ears of that mule—he himself can't be seen—reabsorb the evening.

The light goes out in my lapels.
It is the hour when the solitary birthing of street lamps begins.
Someone turns the switch to the stars.
Which is what we have not proposed to prove.

*From the Spanish. Written in 1925.*

# Lucille and Her Three Fish

Every year, in the month of April, three red fish, three Japanese fish, crossed and uncrossed in silent spirals over Lucille's sweet face. Her graceful forehead, until then without clouds or wayward comets, was marked with three gentle waves.

One fine day, at the beginning of last spring, one of the fish disappeared, the one Lucille had named "Weaver of Dreams."

And when autumn arrived, the second Japanese fish disappeared, one "Horn of Waves," as we, Lucille's friends, used to call him amid polite smiles.

Lucille's forehead returned to the way it was before, a spring from the bottom up: for the third fish, "Silent Winder of Wishes," also wasn't . . . THERE.

When Lucille, with her little mouth painted in the shape of a heart, says "THERE," deliciously half-closing her left eye, in her right eye, as in a fishbowl, the shadow of the third Japanese fish drifts past, somnambulistically—the shadow of "Silent Winder of Wishes."

*From the Spanish. Written in 1925.*

# Deluge

It rained.

It rained in torrents.

Even more than torrentially. It poured oceanically: no one could have imagined that a sea could travel like that, like an airplane, from one planet to another. The atmosphere was transformed into a sea without fish. Soon the fish could calmly leave their tanks and swim into the great aquatic ball of the former atmosphere. Many of them had already stuck their heads out of one body of water and into the next, and stayed that way, with childlike meekness, like half-submerged crocodiles.

The entire city, sheltered under tiled roofs, found itself powerless against the deluge, which fell in slow motion as in dreams, appearing so dense that it didn't fall so much as remain in place.

The whole city, with its great towers dismantled, was an immense brigantine shipwrecked for the first time in the rain.

It rained.

The fish were drawn like moths to the humid light of the street lamps, and on the rooftops the tiles began to open like limpets.

In the shop windows, whole colonies of books searched for something in the water, their pages vibratile and undulating, like the sex of a polyp.

Children swam in the illuminated aquariums of apartments, approaching the windowpanes — a few silly ones — eyes wide, letting a column of tiny circles rise from their round mouths.

It rained. It rained. It rained.

Everything was or soon would be pulsating like an octopus. Everything was repugnant to look at and to touch.

The avenues began to fill up with bloated bellies, swollen bellies toward which, with monstrous voracity, hungry hands, hungry tongues, hungry heads of hair rushed in droves.

At a thousand feet passed the phantasmal light of a wounded streetcar hounded by dolphins, and pierced by millions of brilliant white teeth.

It rained. It rained. It rained. It rained.

Everywhere, between clefts in the water and glaucous radiance, lurked gray eyes with a metallic gaze, with the ferocity of sharks, the eyes of every inhabitant of the city, all eyes, all ferocity.

My ten fingers had no bones, and my eyes, my eyes too watched me stealthily from a distance, larger than ever, forever gray, with the ferocity of all the other eyes.

Not far from me, my drowned bride floated by, propelled by the quivering of her wedding veil, medusa of love and death.

It rained. It rained. It rained. It rained.

The cathedral clock struck the twelve bubbles of midnight.

It rained.

*From the Spanish. Written in 1925.*

# Ramuneta at the Beach

Ramuneta was often told: "The *Venus de Milo* would be interesting if they dressed her in a green silk bathing suit. But you, Ramuneta, with your two blonde braids, would look better in a sky-blue silk bathing suit."

And now—a doe at the seaside—she cavorts on the beach, hugged by an adolescently, tenderly modeled blue bathing suit, resplendent dissembler of her plastic grace, harmonized across the lines of her perfect little body by the budding pegs of her breasts.

"Ramunetaaaa. . . ."

She stops short, enchanted, entranced by my "Ramuneta," with the attention children have for the kites they send out over the beaches.

"Ramuneta, don't you hear the accordions playing in the harbors? Look: right over there, on the bay—is it a breeze or a polka, this sweet sound, this touch that comes to us now?"

But she only giggles and starts dancing around like a silly girl.

How troubling it is, this *Do you want to?* of her thighs and *I can't* of her eyes! From what uncreated gull, from what startling dolphin did she learn such strange poses?

But a decadent sun, enraged by his forced absence, throws one last great handful of rays at her.

"Oh, I can't see, I've just gone blind! Where are we?"

To let her know, I read some lines prepared a few days ago.

Concave diurnal splendor: pure curve that leads to all beaches.

Upon your forehead, Ramuneta, an annelid of light, and beneath your bare feet a navy blue sculpts friezes without knowing it.

An assembly of waves dashes onto the sand of gold: discophorous, the fine undulations: platyhelminthic, the green seaweed. As evening comes without shadows or sounds the sea foam keeps a white rhythm.

A subtle geometry of faraway cities envelopes the horizon in delirious mirages.

A hundred paths suggest a hundred different reasons.

Countryside cities whirlwinds of things and reflections: the world seems to glimpse itself in a local interposition of chromatic aberration.

And before us a sea without ships a sea without fish a sea without beaches a sea without a sea.

Your two blonde braids, Ramuneta, are two exclamation marks lit by the dawn that gives birth to your smile, your smile that steals into my white clothes.

A few moments later, fleeing my appeals, Ramuneta, unsinkable above the two delicious pumpkins of her breasts, was swimming away laughing toward the islands.

*From the Spanish. Written in 1926.*

# Cavalleria rusticana

In the midst of the truncated evening with neither landscape nor a remote moon, a dry tree twitched its imploring branches, stretching them out to the unyielding mirror of the sky, which reproduced that atrocious gesture into infinity.

On the unbroken cord of the horizon, three motionless shepherds, with neither conscience nor staff, formed an enigmatic vignette in the incredible dusk.

Why don't the two subtle oars of evening—light and shadows—cleave the air and stylize forms?

Desolation sobbed falteringly, and in the farthest corner of the heavens a star was breathing its last.

Neither a house, nor a flight, nor a brook.

We were three siblings. Him, Her, and Me.

HIM = HER
HER = ME
HIM = ME

We were triplets. In our house, crystal kisses never flowered on our foreheads. It is sad and humiliating to talk about it, but we were three parthenogenetic triplets.

Here is what happened one evening, or rather on *that* truncated evening with neither landscape nor a remote moon.

For a long time, until she almost lost sight of him, my sister, leaning out from the gothic window, the single solitary light in the room, bade him farewell with the soft caress of her handkerchiefs. Then she sat near the fireplace and there, spinning, diluted the hours with her glances, always with a murmur of brooks, her glances ever chaste, as befitted her status as a maiden.

Nevertheless, on her heart weighed the dark presentiment of evening, with the monotonous and inexorable oscillation of a pendulum.

Suddenly, the garden barked. Someone was marching down the avenue.

Ah! . . . Finally.

HE had returned. It was a tad past six. But he had returned without HER. Where had he left her? What had he done with her gentle cheer? What somber minute had united HER forever with the hermetic evening, as chilling, as irremediable as the past?

Terrified, holding my breath, I watched him enter without asking him. The day's last death rattle still trembled in his eyes.

My brother dropped his old Arabian rifle in a corner and began to sob in front of the fire.

Dear God, what anguish!

"Brother, is it possible that you . . . HER, our sister . . ."

Letting out no cry, still he writhed in pain. A flood of tears rolled down his face, but before falling to the ground they pooled on his cheeks, on his chest. They were hot tears, tears of wax, and repentance trembled as vividly as a flame above his head. He had already completely melted like a thick candle.

Bound together, shoulder to shoulder, the shadows of night entered the room.

*From the Spanish. Written in 1927.*

# The Pleasant Orders of St. Huesca

A question followed by a cannon shot.

"I haven't given the word yet," said the governor.

"Well, that's your business, and for greater security, watch." The governor takes his pill, and sees the following:

Two hours later, along the road from San Feliu y San Guixols walks a piece of roasted meat, weighing about five pounds, fat and charred. I can still see it now, and without compunction I can call it "daughter of a bitch." But she neither moved, nor argued, nor vomited; she could care less.

The road disappears on the horizon in an obstinately straight line, dusty, illuminated by the summer heat. The sight of it gives a feeling of certain opera performances at the moment when a lady in the loge raises her lorgnette to her eyes.

Meanwhile, the roasted meat continues on its way, thinking about nothing in particular. Only a tiny cloud of dust marks its passing. Suddenly an immense multitude, a trillion tiny tailors, the tallest of them less than a sixteenth of an inch, sprouts from the soil, attracted by the sun. Some jump three feet off the ground, others chase after a stray peasant woman, others burn like a wick, and others take up a collection.

The piece of meat, vexed and vomiting, accelerates to a swift run, trampling scores of tailors in its path. After half an hour, the road is nothing more than an immense slough: each tailor dissolves in a drop of urine, disheveled, sobbing, and desperately clutching at the posts along the way before melting into the dust. In the midst of this chaos, from all across the horizon come the echoes of organs, and prayers, and hymns from faraway cathedrals.

The piece of meat has accelerated to a swift run. At a bend in the road, two bumpkins start to grow out of its ears. At the next curve is a cypress tree, and the piece of meat stops in front of it. It rests and looks around.

Exactly three feet away from the base of the cypress, it discerns a shape that immediately goes on the defensive. The piece of meat knows that this is something that can have an influence on the life of the city. It is a running ticktock that now leaps, now asks questions, now also concentrates, wielding a book, or overturns a streetcar onto the heads of the crowd. It'll have nothing to do with agonies or with history. After all, it goes where the people go.

The piece of meat keeps looking around.

The summary pleas of the cypress are rare. Its chambers are covered with steel valves, of vegetal coloration, and its floor is made of frozen meat, which produces such a loud clatter that birds flee the roofs. The clatter isn't heard because it is smaller than a black cat, and just as silent.

The piece of meat sees this as a unique opportunity. Nevertheless, it waits until dawn to go into action.

Meanwhile, the ticktock, leaning in an arc against the ground, distends itself and launches vertically into space. As it ascends, it inflates, grows round. Soon it is nothing more than a cotton cover spread out on the most miserable of beds.

It is eight o'clock, and a student gets ready to go to class.

The piece of meat, next to the font of holy water, offers the sacred liquor to the first of the devout. In the afternoon, all the mules in the city turn up dead in their stables. Someone goes to sprinkle it with gasoline. Suddenly, a cry of horror ( . . . ) One of the onlookers approaches the piece of meat and puts his hand into the piece of meat's washbowl.

After a great effort he succeeds in pulling out a voluminous book of oblique songs. On its cover, in ornate letters, appears the title

The Life of St. Huesca

A short while later, a sacristan loads a donkey with earthen pitchers at the foot of the church ruins. In each pitcher hides a bandit who, upon arriving in the forest, will leap from his hiding place and together with his companions build a hut. In the hut there will be a whore. The whore will go to a cypress, the cypress on a windy day will attract maidens who will offer it their bottoms. The maidens' bottoms will then be trampled by the piece of meat, who will sing while it tramples, and its canticle will be as the glug-glug of water that restores sight to the blind. ( . . . )

The governor is on his feet now, witnessing the passing of St. Huesca, who walks to martyrdom with her head lowered. Her hand wields a palm. Behind her, half-crushed under a rain of stones, crawls a black cat that is going deaf. On the cross upon which they crucified St. Huesca there hangs, indifferent, sheeplike, made into a lector, the piece of roasted meat.

*Inscription for the piece of meat's tombstone*

Two children were walking in a bell tower without giving thought to how beneficial their obligations were, when all of a sudden they seemed to hear everything that was going on at school. Immediately climbing to the top of a cypress, they could observe the following: Two Marists, prepared to risk their lives, were riding on a streetcar. They got off at the first stop and took another streetcar, full of bee-hives. The bees made a wonderful noise and the Marists laid themselves to rest in their coffins, prepared to risk everything. One of them said under his breath, "Is it true, as Péret said, that mortadella is made by the blind?" And the other answered, "We've arrived at the footbridge." Beneath the footbridge, in the middle of the half-putrefied, half-green water, a gravestone could be seen that read, "The Norms." All around, hundreds of people were celebrating the New Year.

That is the gravestone that the piece of meat must have for 364 days in an ordinary year and 365 during leap year.

*From the Spanish. Written in 1927.*

# Letter to Pepín Bello
# on St. Valero's Day


*Madrid, February 2, 1927*

My dear Pepín: How touched I was upon reading your letter and seeing with what modesty you recall that unforgettable day of the 29th, the day on which St. Valero the Windy passes with a window arched above his head on the sidewalk of Cecilio Gasca!* You were always very good and have remembered to observe the 29th. I, on the contrary, decided to go for a checkup on St. Valero's Day. I'm not well. I'm losing strength every day. When the doctor began to ausculcate me, a great wind broke loose outside, a storm so brutal that it tore the shutters off the balcony as if they were arms. The dust in the street was so dense that you couldn't even see the priests go by. Spinning rapidly in the dust, flashing for an instant before vanishing into the void, were an infinite number of sewing machines, canes, funnel-shaped washbasins, and small Formosa islands surrounded by schools of tuna.

Neither my father nor the doctor understood anything of this.

My good father objected that this gust of wind represented a serious stumbling block in his life, and that he would not for a moment tolerate such an indecent diagnosis. The doctor said that might be so, but that my forebear always had to one-up him, and that for all his much-vaunted experience, he, the doctor, was nonetheless greater, and he could find another sucker for that story.

---

*[Pepín Bello, a Spanish surrealist, was a friend of Buñuel's in the residence hall at the University of Madrid. St. Valero is the patron saint of Zaragoza.— Trans.]

My father grabbed my hand and pulled me into the street. The violence of the wind was at its height. Such a strong smell of wax! A contemptible humming stunned us, and large and mighty gusts would barely let us move ahead. The tornado knocked us senseless, hurling in our faces hundreds of half-naked priests. I noticed that all of them, when striking our noses, would start singing through clenched teeth, and always the same song. It was something like this motet:

> Little girl, my little girl,
> you don't know what is the sea;
> if you knew, my life, my pearl,
> you'd roll over instantly.

The moral of the story might seem frivolous, but it reminded me of when I was a waiter, and my poor father would come to bring me couscous at the cafe, a little before noon, on an unforgettable little gold plate, which he would always leave a couple of miles from the tables.

There kept appearing more and more priests to crash into our noses. The song became a drone, almost unintelligible, which suddenly made me see that it contained a less than respectful allusion to my absent mother. But tell me, Pepín, who takes offense because capitals stop being made in this or that style? To hell with them!

Finally, the cassock of one of the priests got trapped in the white and venerable mustache of my father. There the priest remained, willing to do anything, the way good people are. He took advantage of the situation, to my great chagrin, by launching into the following diatribe:

"In truth, I say to you, my son, St. Valero never failed to respect the code. The art of his time—and I say this to you without rancor—consisted of dispelling the static hum of great ships from which only the smoke of battles could rise. There, the errant breasts, the wings of stone, the sad furrows, the carefree snacks over tombstones, the incests, the stray sentences heard in the night, and the woodpiles stacked by the hands of children!

"Now then, St. Valero, seated opposite the till, never wanted for a single dime. He, his father, his grandfather, all were accountants, and furthermore engineers. Too bad that St. Valero's son, also called St. Valero, didn't have the means to pay for his studies. But that's in the next chapter."

At these last words, night fell. The priest fell silent, and with skillfulness and love, he began herding his scattered goats; once the herd had regrouped, he made it venture down the steep slope that led into the valley.

### Very important

Around the valley winds a wall, which I could not cross. Ten enormous priests with powerful scimitars prevented me from entering. On the shining blades of their weapons, I could make out the following inscription: "Around the valley winds a wall." The last word, half-effaced, was hard to discern. Did it say *wall* or perhaps *wake?* Perhaps it was neither *wall* nor *wake*, but rather a photograph of *The Last Supper*, in which the table guests have been replaced by ciboria, and the ciborium seated in Christ's place whacks the ciborium inclining its head on his shoulder with a bottle, and the last ciborium—the one who plays Judas—holds a dray in his hand.

I became angry. "Are ye priests or gentiles? If the former, let us fight; if the latter, may God give you your deserts."

But already at dusk, the valley, the vigil, the scimitars are no more than the drumming of a typewriter, manipulated by the head stenographer himself. He removes the paper from the carriage, puts it in an envelope, and, by hand, writes the address in pencil:

Mr. Altalicio Pantaléon
    Palatino Pudibondo
    PANTICOSA

Write me.

### Realistic details

My sister admits that St. Valero's Day was very strange in Zaragoza: "San Pablo Street was filled with people one wouldn't normally see there—barons, countesses, the Parellada matrons with large hats! Then, to enter the Church of San Pablo, you'd go down some stairs, and inside, on a frail altar, was St. Valero, who is a swarthy saint with a raised finger and a ring of candles. Finally, at home we would eat a St. Valero made of sugar, and everyone was very happy and very sad. Perhaps because on that day our grandfather died."

*From the Spanish. Written in 1927.*

# Idea for a Story

It has to do with a soirée I throw at my house that ends catastrophically. I find myself obliged to go to the house of a wise friend, where "big things" happen. From there, I end up at the Hospital of Outer Toledo, where again lots of things happen. At last I die, not without first making a will—wait till you see this will!—and, finally . . .

No sooner said than done, so that I might have the time to die decently. Four gravediggers take hold of my body, carrying me to the church next door to get on with my burial. Lifting the foul stone of Cardinal Tavera's sepulcher, pulling out his vile carrion, which they had to throw onto a dungheap because not even the poor wanted it, they placed me there for eternity.

May loincloths rest in peace!

*From the Spanish. Written in 1927.*

# La Sancta Misa Vaticanae

*La Sancta Misa Vaticanae*, read the title in macaronic Latin. There would be a short film showing a competition of masses in St. Peter's plaza in Rome. The Church, "always attentive to the conquests of civilization and sports," thought to set the mass to the pulsating rhythm of our time. To that end, functional altars are placed between every pair of gigantic pillars in the plaza designed by Bernini, with a priest officiating at each. At the word "go," the priests begin to say mass as fast as they can. They reach incredible speeds at turning toward the faithful to say the Dominus vobiscum, making the sign of the cross, etc., while the altar boy goes back and forth with the missal and the other ritual objects. A few fall down exhausted, like boxers. Finally, Mosén Rendueles, of Huesca, is declared the winner, having said the entire mass in a record one minute and forty-five seconds. As a prize he receives a monstrance and a large Aragonian wicker basket.

*From the Spanish. Written in 1927.*

# Menage à trois

However much I tried, I couldn't see the face of the chauffeur, some kind of cossack driving our car. Next to me traveled a woman in mourning with the distinction of a goddess and the pallor of dawn. I didn't know her. I had never seen her before. But I felt my skin awakening, drenched in lust. We traversed a skyless landscape, skyless as far as the eye could see. The ground was covered with black flowers that gave off the penetrating scent of a boudoir.

My unknown woman ordered the chauffeur to stop at a large full lake, a tear duct filled with anguish. "This," she told me, "is the full lachrymal lake of anguish." I took little notice, occupied as I now was with kissing her between her breasts, which she concealed with her hands, crying inconsolably, almost without the strength to fend off my lascivious advances.

The chauffeur came up to us with his cap in his hand, I don't know what for. I thought I recognized his face, and all doubt as to his identity disappeared when, with a smile, he exclaimed, "Lake, my friend." Overjoyed, I responded, "It's you, my old lachrymal lake friend." We greeted each other with exhilaration, embracing with such joy as at the resurrection of the dead.

A funeral procession had just stopped nearby. Shrouded in the coffin lay the unknown woman of a few moments before. Pale flower of flesh that could no longer sing! Her last tear still slid down her cheek, suspended miraculously on her cheekbone like a bird on a branch.

My friend fell upon her and kissed her frantically on the lips, lips that though livid imperceptibly turned green, then red, then into fire, then into hell.

I began to feel a mortal hatred of the chauffeur, who was no longer my friend. I began to feel a limitless revulsion for that taste of lemon in flames that must have lingered on his lips, left by the unburied lips of the unknown woman.

*From the Spanish. Written in 1927.*

# A Decent Story

Little Carmen was very docile. Carmencita's innocence was proverbial. Her mother watched over her night and day, placing before her daughter the wall of her vigilance against the snares of the world. When Carmencita turned twelve, her mother became extremely worried. "The day my daughter menstruates *for the first time*," she thought, "goodbye to her golden innocence." But she found a way to solve the problem. When she saw Carmencita turn pale for the *first time*, she rushed into the street like a madwoman and soon returned with a large bunch of red flowers. "Here, my daughter, take these; now you are about to become a woman." And Carmencita, beguiled and delighted by those marvelous red flowers, forgot to have her period. Each month, twelve times a year for many years, Carmencita was fooled in the same way and kept from the vile truth. As soon as the shadows appeared beneath her eyes before the thirtieth of every month, her mother placed the red flowers in her hands.

Carmencita turned forty. Her mother, now very old, still called her Carmencita, though everyone else called her Doña Carmela. At that age there came a month when the shadows did not appear beneath Carmencita's eyes, and so her mother gave her a bouquet of white flowers. "Here, my daughter, this is the last bouquet I offer you, now that you have ceased to be a woman." Carmencita was indignant. "But Mama, I never even knew I was one." To which her mother responded, "So much the worse for you, my daughter." It was that white bouquet, now withered, its petals falling, scattered and dry, that they placed on Carmencita's coffin.

### An Indecent Story

As for Little Mary, when the critical age arrived, her mother wanted to do what Little Carmen's mother had done, and when she saw her become pallid, with shadows under her eyes, she gave her a bouquet of red roses. But Mariquita was much more brazen than Carmencita. She took the bouquet, opened the window, threw out the flowers, and began to menstruate.

*From the Spanish. Written in 1927.*

# On Love

I. What sort of hopes do you place in love?

L.B.: If I'm in love, all hopes. If not, none.

II. How do you view the transition from the *idea of love* to *the fact of being in love?* Willingly or otherwise, would you sacrifice your freedom to love? Have you ever done so? Would you consent, if you felt it necessary in order to be worthy of love, to sacrifice a cause that up to that point you had considered yourself bound to defend? Would you agree not to become what you might have been, if at that price you could fully savor the certainty of love? How would you judge a man who would go so far as to betray his convictions to please the woman he loves? Can such a pledge be asked of him, and obtained?

L.B.: 1. For me, nothing exists but the fact of being in love.
2. I would gladly sacrifice my freedom to love. I have already done so.
3. I would sacrifice a cause for the sake of love, but that remains to be seen in the moment.
4. Yes.
5. I would judge him very favorably. But nevertheless, I would ask that man not to betray his convictions. I would even go so far as to insist on it.

III. Would you acknowledge the right to deprive yourself for a time of the presence of the person you love, knowing how exhilarating absence can be for love, yet aware of the mediocrity of such a strategy?

L.B.: I would not wish to separate myself from the loved one. At any price.

IV. Do you believe in the victory of admirable love over sordid life, or that of sordid life over admirable love?

L.B.: I don't know.

*From the French. Interview published in* La Révolution surréaliste, *no. 12, December 15, 1929.*

# A Giraffe

This giraffe, life-sized, is a simple board cut in the shape of a giraffe, with a peculiarity that sets it apart from other animals of its kind made of wood. Each of its spots, which from ten or twelve feet away look perfectly ordinary, is actually formed either by a lid that each viewer can easily open by rotating it on a small hinge placed invisibly on one side, or by an object, or by a hole revealing the light of day—the giraffe is only a few inches thick—or by a concavity containing the various objects detailed in the following list.

It should be noted that this giraffe doesn't make complete sense until its full potential is realized, that is to say, until each of its spots performs the function for which it was intended. If this realization is extremely costly, it is not, for all that, any less possible.

### Everything Is Absolutely Realizable

To conceal whatever objects are behind the animal, it must be placed in front of a black wall thirty-five feet high and a hundred and thirty feet long. The surface of the wall must be intact. In front of this wall, a garden of asphodels needs to be kept up, one with the same measurements as those of the wall.

### What Must Be Found in Each of the Giraffe's Spots

*In the first:* the interior of the spot comprises a small, quite complicated mechanism resembling that of a watch. In the midst of the turning of cogwheels, a small propeller spins vertiginously. The whole gives off a faint cadaver smell. After having moved away from the spot, pick up an album that should be found on the ground at the giraffe's feet. Sit down in a corner of the garden and leaf through the album, which shows dozens of photos of very miserable, tiny and deserted plazas. They are those of various Castilian old towns: Alba de Tormes, Soria, Madrigal de las Altas Torres, Orgaz, Burgo de Osma, Tordesillas, Simancas, Sigüenza, Cadalso de los Vidrios, and above all Toledo.

*In the second:* on the condition that it is opened at noon, as specified in the inscription on the outside, we find ourselves in the presence of a cow's eye in its socket, with eyelashes and eyelid. The image of the viewer is reflected in the eye. The eyelid must suddenly close, putting an end to our contemplation.

*In the third:* upon opening this spot, we read, against a red velvet background, these two words:

Américo Castro*

The letters being detachable, we can give ourselves over to rearranging them in all possible combinations.

*In the fourth:* there is a small grate, like that of a prison. Through the grate, we hear a real orchestra of one hundred musicians playing the overture to *Die Meistersinger.*

*In the fifth:* two billiard balls fall with a great clatter as soon as the spot is opened. Inside, nothing is left but a rolled-up parchment, standing upright and tied with a string. Unroll it in order to read this poem:

*To Richard the Lionhearted*

From the choir to the cellar, from the cellar to the hill, from the hill
    to hell, to the black mass of winter's death throes.

---

*[A professor at the University of Madrid, where he was Buñuel's adviser, Castro was a onetime ambassador to Berlin.—Trans.]

From the choir to the sex of the she-wolf who fled in the timeless
   forest of the Middle Ages.
*Verba vedata sunt fodido en culo et puto gafo*, it was the taboo of the
   first hut erected in the infinite woods, it was the taboo of the
   evacuation of the goat from which sprang the hordes who raised
   the cathedrals.
Blasphemies floated in the bogs, peat trembled beneath the whips of
   the maimed bishops of marble, we used female genitals to fashion
   toads.
With time the nuns revived, green branches sprouted from their dry
   sides, the incubuses winked at them while soldiers pissed on the
   convent walls and centuries swarmed in the lepers' sores.
From the windows hung clusters of dry nuns who produced, with
   the help of a warm spring wind, a sweet murmur of prayer.
I will have to pay my share, Richard the Lionhearted, *fodido en
   puto gafo.*

*In the sixth:* the spot passes right through the giraffe. We gaze at
the landscape through the hole; some thirty feet away, my mother—
Mrs. Buñuel—dressed as a laundress, kneels beside a small brook wash-
ing clothes. A few cows behind her.

*In the seventh:* a simple piece of cloth from an old sack soiled with
plaster.

*In the eighth:* this spot is slightly concave and covered with very fine,
curly blond hair taken from the pubis of a young adolescent Danish girl
with very light blue eyes, a plump body with sunburned skin, all inno-
cence and candor. The viewer must blow softly on the hairs.

*In the ninth:* in place of the spot we discover a large, dark moth with
a death's-head between its wings.

*In the tenth:* on the inside of the spot is a substantial amount of dough.
One is tempted to knead it between one's fingers. The blades of a well-
hidden razor will bloody the hands of the viewer.

*In the eleventh:* a pork bladder membrane replaces the spot. Nothing
more. Take the giraffe and carry it to Spain, and set it at the place called

Masada del Vicario, four miles from Calanda, in southern Aragón, its head pointed north. Burst the membrane with your fist and look through the hole. You will see a very poor cottage, whitewashed, in the midst of a desert landscape. In the foreground, a fig tree is placed a few feet from the door. In the background, bare mountains and olive trees. At this moment an old plowman will perhaps come out of the house, barefoot.

*In the twelfth:* a very beautiful photo of the head of Christ with a crown of thorns, but ROARING WITH LAUGHTER.

*In the thirteenth:* deep inside the spot, a very beautiful, larger-than-life rose composed of apple peels. The androecium is made of bloody meat. The rose will turn black a few hours later. It will go rotten the next day. Three days later, a legion of worms will appear on its remains.

*In the fourteenth:* a black hole. We hear this conversation whispered with great anguish:

WOMAN'S VOICE: *No, I beg you. Don't freeze.*

MAN'S VOICE: *Yes, I must. I would not be able to look you in the eye* (we hear the sound of rain).

WOMAN'S VOICE: *I love you all the same, I'll always love you, but* don't freeze. DO . . . NOT . . . FREEZE. (Pause.)

MAN'S VOICE (very low, very soft): *My little cadaver . . .* (Pause. We hear a stifled laugh.)

A very bright light abruptly illuminates the interior of the spot. In this light, we see several hens pecking.

*In the fifteenth:* a small window with a double casement constructed in perfect imitation of a large one. Suddenly a thick puff of white smoke bursts from it, followed, some seconds later, by a distant explosion. (The smoke and explosion must be like those from a cannon, seen and heard from a few miles away.)

*In the sixteenth:* upon opening the spot, we see about ten feet away Fra Angelico's *Annunciation*, very well framed and lit, but in pitiful condition: shredded with a knife, sticky with pitch, the image of the Virgin carefully spattered with excrement, her eyes gouged out with needles, the sky bearing in large letters the inscription: DOWN WITH THE MOTHER OF THE TURK.

*In the seventeenth:* a powerful jet of steam will gush from the spot at the moment it opens and horribly blind the viewer.

*In the eighteenth:* the opening of the spot provokes the harrowing fall of the following objects: needles, thread, a thimble, pieces of fabric, two empty matchboxes, a piece of candle, a very old deck of cards, a few buttons, empty flasks, grains of the Valleys, a square watch, a door handle, a broken pipe, two letters, orthopedic apparatuses, and a few live spiders. All are scattered in the most disturbing way. (This spot is the only one that symbolizes death.)

*In the nineteenth:* behind the spot, a model less than three feet square representing the Sahara Desert under a crushing light. Covering the sand, a hundred thousand miniature Marists made of wax, their white aprons detaching from their cassocks. In the heat, the Marists melt little by little. (Many millions of Marists must be kept on reserve.)

*In the twentieth:* we open this spot. Arranged on four boards we see twelve tiny terra-cotta busts of Madame . . . ,* exquisite likenesses, though only about three-quarters of an inch tall. Under a magnifying glass, we can see that the teeth are made of ivory. The last little bust has all its teeth pulled.

*From the French. Published in* Le Surréalisme au service de la révolution, *no. 6, May 15, 1933.*

*I cannot reveal this name.

# AN ANDALUSIAN DOG

[The English title refers to Buñuel's book
*Un Perro andaluz* (1927), rather than to the film
*Un Chien andalou* (1928). See page 258.
—Trans.]

# For Myself I Would Like

Tears or willow on the ground
teeth of gold
teeth of pollen
like the mouth of a girl
from whose hair swells a river
in each drop a tiny fish
in each tiny fish a gold tooth
in each gold tooth a fifteen-year-old smile,
that dragonflies may reproduce

What can a maiden think about
when the wind discovers her thighs?

*From the Spanish. Written in 1927.*

# Miraculous Polisher

In winter the cries of the semaphores fall into the sea
riddled with wind and crucifixion
A ship can wreck in a drop of my blood
of my blood when it falls on the breast
of a Louis XV marquise of foam

That landscape freezes less in the mirror
than in the fingernails of the dead
who come back to life
with fingers transformed into flowers
into flowers of extinct agony and of salvation.

Divided like a valley of Jehoshaphat
the part on my head waits for them.
While Christ condemns
the Virgin Mary in a white dressing gown
will give a piece of bread to the condemned
and place a bird of caresses
on the brow of the saved.

*From the Spanish. Written in 1927.*

# It Seems to Me
# Neither Good nor Evil

I think they watch us from time to time
from the front from the back from the sides
the rancorous eyes of hens
more dreadful than the putrefied water of grottoes
incestuous as the eyes of the mother
who died on the gallows
viscous as coitus
as the gelatin swallowed by vultures

I think I will have to die
with hands buried in the mire of roads

I think that if a son were born to me
he would remain eternally watching
the beasts copulating in the late afternoon.

*From the Spanish. Written in 1927.*

# Upon Getting into Bed

The remains of the star caught in your hair
crackled like peanut shells
the star whose light you had already discovered
a million years ago
in the precise instant of the birth
of a tiny Chinese infant

"THE CHINESE ARE THE ONLY ONES WHO DO NOT FEAR
THE GHOSTS
THAT RISE FROM OUR PORES EVERY NIGHT AT MIDNIGHT."

It's a pity that the star
couldn't fertilize your breasts
and that the bird of the oil lamp
pecked at it like a peanut shell
your glances and mine left in your womb
a luminous, future sign of multiplication.

*From the Spanish. Written in 1927.*

# The Rainbow and the Poultice

How many Marists can fit on a footbridge?
Four or five?
How many eighth notes does a Don Juan have?
1,230,424
These questions are easy.

Are the keys lice?
Can I catch cold on the thighs of my lover?
Will the Pope excommunicate pregnant women?
Does a policeman know how to sing?
Are hippopotamuses happy?
Are pederasts sailors?
And these questions, are they just as easy?

In a few moments two salivas
will go down the street
leading an academy of deaf-mute children by the hand.

Would it be impolite of me to vomit a piano on them
from my balcony?

*From the Spanish. Written in 1927.*

# Redemptress

I found myself in the snow-covered garden of a monastery. From a nearby cloister a Benedictine monk gazed upon me curiously, holding a large red mastiff by a chain. I had the feeling that the friar wanted to turn him loose on me, and filled with fear I began to dance in the snow. Slowly at first. Then, increasingly as the hatred welled in the eyes of my viewer, with fury, like a madman, like someone possessed. All the blood rushed to my head, blinding my eyes with red, the very same red of the mastiff. The friar finally disappeared, and the snow melted. Then, through wheat fields bathed in the light of spring, came my sister dressed in white, bringing me a turtledove in her upraised hands. It was exactly noon, the moment at which every priest on earth raises the Host over the wheat.

I greeted my sister with my arms crossed on my chest, completely delivered, in the midst of the white, august silence of the Host.

*From the Spanish. Published in* Gaceta literaria, *no. 50, January 15, 1929.*

# Bacchanal

Mutton at 125 pesetas
rippled abundant pliant as the belly
of a woman at 150 pesetas
the bread eaten by the poor
can be kneaded with that belly
and baked with a fire of thumbs

When we form a cross with our thumbs
we renew the martyrdom of St. Bartholomew
who it was later known was a faun
or a member
shrinking in front of the cross

St. Bartholomew and the faun were dancing when
rocks shot up from the ground
like kisses blown from fingertips
Upon dying he was eaten by joyful ants
that were not really ants
but a few silent dancers

From the tomb of St. Bartholomew
sprouts an ear of burning meat
for every kiss he could but would not steal.

*From the Spanish. Published in* Gaceta literaria, *no. 50, January 15, 1929.*

# Odor of Sanctity

Someone gave me a fatal shove. I began to slide away at a vertiginous speed on a vertiginous toboggan. Accelerating mathematically. Interplanetarily. Turned at forty-five degrees with the sensation of having been changed into one of those screws let loose by the stars that turn a million times a second. All a vortex, turns, hisses, shouts, arrow shots, stomach in the throat, hurrahs from the crowd, glory, suspension, fright, cold.

I'm going to crash! I'm going to crash!

But I never got to the end of my fall. I felt more and more out of control, like a toboggan within the toboggan.

A top spinning to the $n^{th}$ power.

The descent of the thermometer column.

The cold of millions of stars piercing the end of my nose.

So exaggerated was the gravitation that I burst out laughing.

"Go on! Go on!" the crowd kept shouting in fury.

Centuries were seconds in that toboggan rifled like a mauser.

When I had finally despaired of finding rest, there came a terrible explosion. The planet Saturn had crashed into a streetcar filled with children.

Suddenly I felt an equatorial languor. An ermine mantle placed lovingly upon my shoulders. A calm through my viscera, which until then had been bristling. Somnolence. A hand or a wing settled on my forehead. And an ancient voice saying, "Now you can die."*

*From the Spanish. Published in* Gaceta literaria, *no. 51, February 1, 1929.*

*[A typed draft of this piece ends with an additional paragraph: "And I sensed death enter, my death, like an infant's first smile."—Trans.]

# Palace of Ice

The puddles formed a decapitated domino of buildings, of which one is the tower they told me about in childhood, with only one window as high up as a mother's eyes as she leans over the cradle.

Near the door a hanged man dangles over the enclosed abyss of eternity, howling for a long while. It's me. It is my skeleton with nothing left now but the eyes. Now they smile at me, now they squint, now THEY ARE GOING TO EAT A CRUMB OF BREAD IN THE INTERIOR OF MY BRAIN. The window opens and a lady appears filing her nails. When she considers them sharp enough she tears out my eyes and throws them into the street.

My empty sockets remain, no gaze, no desires, no sea, no little chicks, no nothing.

A nurse comes in and sits down next to me at the cafe table. She unfolds a newspaper from 1856 and reads in an emotional voice:

"When Napoleon's soldiers entered Zaragoza, VILE Zaragoza, they found nothing but wind blowing through the deserted streets. Alone in a puddle croaked the eyes of Luis Buñuel. Napoleon's soldiers finished them off with bayonets."

*From the Spanish. Published in* Helix *(Vilafranca del Penedés), no. 4, May 1929.*

# Bird of Anguish

A plesiosaur slept between my eyes
while music burned in a lamp
and the landscape felt the passion of Tristan and Isolde.

Your body fit into mine
like a hand fits around whatever it wants to hide;
flayed
it showed me your muscles of wood
and the bouquets of lust
that could be made from your veins.

We heard the gallop of bison in heat
in our skin trembling like the leaves of a garden;
all conversations about love are the same,
all have their delirious chords,
but the heart crushed
by a music of secular memories;
later come prayer and the wind,
the wind that twists sounds into a point
of a sweetness of blood,
of howls become flesh.

What longing, what desires of shattered seas
changed into nickel
or into an ecumenical song of what could have been a tragedy,

will be born, birds of our coupled mouths,
while death enters through our feet?

Suspended like a bridge of stone kisses, one o'clock struck.
Two flew by with hands crossed over its chest.
Three sounded farther away than death.
Four was already trembling with dawn.
Five traced with a compass the circular transmitter of day.

At six could be heard the little goats of the Alps
led to the altar by monks.

*From the Spanish. Published in* Helix *(Vilafranca del Penedés), no. 4, May 1929.*

# THEATER

# Hamlet

(A Comic Tragedy)

## Dramatis Personae

HAMLET   *Lover of the upper part of Leticia*

AGRIFONTE   *Hamlet's rival. Lover of Leticia's interesting spot*

MITHRADATES   *Recalcitrant cadaver*

DON LUPO   *Dance instructor*

HAMLET'S FATHER   *Docile and well-mannered ghost*

THE COMPANION FOR LIFE

A CAPTAIN

LETICIA   *Nominative of* Letitia, -ae

MARGARITA   *Lovesick Moorish woman*

COURTIERS AND SOLDIERY

NOTE: At the end of each act, the peasants will be foreshadowed.

## Act I

*(A nondescript field. Here and there little streams choked with tears. In the distance, the Cathedral of Rouen before anyone laid hands on it. On the horizon a crazy boy declines* musa, musae.*)*

AGRIFONTE  As I was saying, Hamlet, my friend, the dead are all the same: all lives are also alike, and the only ones that differ are those that can be proven like a theorem. Tell me, what's become of Margarita?

HAMLET Margarita? Which Margarita? The one who spangles sunny meadows or the ill-fated, deep-voiced one who fainted into your arms?

AGRIFONTE The one who gave us this cigarette case. *(He offers Hamlet a cigarette.)* Here, have one, I pray you.

HAMLET Thank you.

AGRIFONTE As God lives, don't light it, or you'll find out who I am.

HAMLET Bah! Just yesterday I got a telegram from your uncle telling me what sort of fellow you are.

AGRIFONTE *(Surprised.)* My uncle? Which one of the seven?

HAMLET The eighth one. The well-documented one, the one who much to his regret could not give you your being.

AGRIFONTE In the name of Christ, tell me, once and for all, who is my mother's son?

HAMLET Well, here goes, though it grieve you. You are Lady Irascible of Alvaro Menor, putative mother of she who once knew incredible diastoles.

AGRIFONTE *(Surly.)* Save your proverbs for later and behold your creation.

*(Hamlet looks in the direction indicated. A frightful tableau imposes itself before him. In a comfortable coffin lies Mithradates, decomposed and episcopal.)*

MITHRADATES *(Sitting up.)* O Hamlet! O Agrifonte! You shall never see Margarita again.

HAMLET AND AGRIFONTE What are you saying, fool, in the midst of such horrible putrefaction?

MITHRADATES Margarita went to the interrogation field. Whoever dares go there never comes back.

HAMLET AND AGRIFONTE O son of a bitch, scoundrel; you are also in love with Margarita.

MITHRADATES  Me? I no longer love nor hate. But Margarita shall be my wife in winged shadows.

*(Hamlet and Agrifonte burn with cosmetic anger. A vindicating sun unsheathes thousands of rays on the horizon. The shadows of the three characters appear stubborn and flattened on the moor.)*

HAMLET AND AGRIFONTE  Pimp, rascal, rot—now you'll see.

*(The two rouse their shadows like hounds. These great black spiders advance toward Mithradates' coffin.)*

MITHRADATES  Ah, you've vanquished me! That was your sole recourse against me. But beware the shadow of my shadow. Death is lighter than sleep.

*(The shadows of the three argue metaphysically, incited by their respective masters. Agrifonte's shadow has Mithradates' by the neck. Hamlet's shadow barks at the moon, scaring it away.)*

*(A pitiless hurricane carries away the three shadows, which disappear gesticulating on the horizon.)*

*(Mithradates dies definitively in the midst of clumsy mechanisms.)*

AGRIFONTE  Now that we don't have shadows, let's be honest: Hamlet, you also love Margarita.

HAMLET  Me? No way.

AGRIFONTE  Well then, why did your shadow attack our poor, lamented Mithradates?

HAMLET  *(Very eighteenth-century.)* For love in general.

AGRIFONTE  Now I understand everything. *(He continues in a heavy foreign accent.)* Hamlet, get ready, I'm going to tell your mom everything.

HAMLET  Go ahead, tell her. But meanwhile I'm keeping the baroque little cardboard horse.

*(Agrifonte exits, playing with his hoop. His mother, embedded in the wall, sheds*

*a distant tear. Four weeping maidens lean over Mithradates' corpse and carry it through the twisted course of the day.)*

## Act II

*(Margarita, alone in the meadow, haphazardly cleans her braids. She sings in a playful, improvised language.)*

MARGARITA

Cridia estroche eka per crilo

Idrios celían tankar

Alora e cor per atores

Non plivía credoyar

*(After swinging in the cathedral, she goes on:)*

That's life so large

A lot of humming

A lot of arithmetic

And very few people

*(Speaking.)* If only Hamlet, my love, were here. But there he is.

*(She hurriedly exchanges the francs she still has, then puts on an adolescent air.)*

HAMLET *(Entering.)* Margarita, have you ever been to the sea?

MARGARITA That's what I was up to, sir, when you got here. But is that all you have to say to me after such a long absence?

HAMLET That's all.

MARGARITA My, how you've changed since your ambiguous trip to Amsterdam. Perhaps the bankers or some other maiden more favorable than I . . .

HAMLET Margarita . . . I could love you . . .

MARGARITA Say it.

HAMLET But it would be impossible to confine my love to your most elevated regions.

MARGARITA  Love me, lord, love me. What does it matter. We can talk about the rest on Monday.

HAMLET  I love only Leticia.

MARGARITA  Love me, lord, you won't regret it. Ask your father's soldiers if by chance they regretted loving me.

HAMLET  Now that you put it that way, let me love you too. I'll begin, if you like, by placing my childish lips on your faraway breasts.

MARGARITA  Begin.

HAMLET  Let's build first.

MARGARITA  Let's build.

*(The two of them build. There are only two bricks left when Hamlet, desperate because Margarita hasn't shown up for their date, loses himself among the rest of the soldiers.)*

### Scene 2

*(Margarita's mansion. She is with her dance instructor, Don Lupo, showily going through a lesson.)*

DON LUPO  One, two. One, two. Now that foot . . . that's right . . . Turn, turn on your favorite heel, but without any frills . . . That's it . . . Stop!

*(The soldiers come to a halt. One of them, an undisciplined soon-to-be captain, steps forward.)*

CAPTAIN  Enough, Don Lupo. You have been accused of being an intellectual. What do you say to that? You lower your head, you don't respond. Say your famous prayer, because you shall perish. Soldiers! Fire at will!

*(A savage shot rings out, then another. Don Lupo, respectably bloodied, blames his horse.)*

DON LUPO  It was nothing, Margarita. My horse, one—on my faith!—ignorant horse, fell on my head as I passed by your window. But when I have you in my arms, who has time to think of polygons and padlocks? Let's take pleasure in our love, Margarita.

MARGARITA *(Aside.)* How dare he? Oh, the vile little teacher, and what a filthy liaison he's proposing. But we must pretend, for the sake of my honor. *(Out loud.)* Sir, we close the store at twelve. Kindly choose your ancestry, for afterward it will be too late.

DON LUPO Fine. I'll take that one, there. The arborescent yellow one sticking out over the lintel.

MARGARITA Which of the two? Rustic or profane?

DON LUPO *(Perversely.)* Whichever you like.

MARGARITA Here you are.

*(She gives it to him, and then offers it to her cousin. Don Lupo, with his ento-mologist's box, shows off his mustache, spread out and active. His great pow-dered and most miserable mustache.)*

### Act III

*(A well-worn dungeon. For God's sake, why is carnival being discussed this year in such a definitive dungeon? Marquises artificially bleed to death along the nauseating walls. Through a tiny squalid window come the last dissolving rays of the day.)*

AGRIFONTE *(Naked and Machiavellian, he dreams out loud.)* Chaste and distant, God celebrated sidereal dances, and the day that had not yet arrived trembled in its genesis. He came and went, braided and unbraided his eternal beard in the golden towers. Now, while this baroque remorse oppresses me, the women must be dancing, the wind in their hair, through the sweet islands of the morning. While my final hour chimes, how their graceful leaps must bend this ineffable autumn afternoon!

*(He rises like a sleepwalker and grabs his companion by the lapels.)*

AGRIFONTE Tell me, have you seen the eyeless stork of the gallows being raised in the Plaza of the Four Corners?

COMPANION Yes. I was forced to replace the executioner after his dismissal. He was too sentimental and took it upon himself to feed the pigeons in the plaza. Tourists stopped to see such a marvel. He was denounced to the governor because of the words he would whisper to them gently, his beak next to theirs: "Pigeons, little pigeons, tiny pigeons, teensy pigeons." It was a stupid phrase, but also tender, and that's what they couldn't excuse.

AGRIFONTE Then you're the one appointed to marry me with the ring of that noose.

COMPANION Yes, it's true. But first . . . You must know something. Margarita and Hamlet have run away together.

AGRIFONTE *(Puzzled.)* Together? *(Red with anger.)* What do you mean?

COMPANION Look. *(He shows him the canoe he has kept hidden behind his back.)*

AGRIFONTE *(Crazed.)* Heavens! Woe is me! I'm cursed! *(He trips iniquitously.)* So the abominable aqueduct . . .

COMPANION *(Sardonically.)* Dead as well.

AGRIFONTE *(Enlightened.)* Then there's still time. Let us reproach at once, and may heaven be with us.

COMPANION Let us reproach, if you think it best.

*(The two mount horses and disappear ecstatically. In a corner, the forgotten canoe gives the scene a sense of infinite sadness, like a dried-up sea, a lunar sea, empty spheres of irreparable dryness.)*


*Scene 2*

*(The outskirts of Amsterdam. Several creatures graze roughly on the meadows.*

*Next to a canal a nauseating archbishop drones equitably. An invisible shepherd rings the white hole of the afternoon.)*

DON LUPO *(Dressed like a shepherd.)* The moon, wounded on the forehead by the round rock of the sun, now wraps itself in a shroud of light. Now my sickly livestock ruminate on silhouettes, and the liberated Agrifonte has yet to arrive. Does he still moan in his horrible cell? But no, here he comes now.

AGRIFONTE *(To Don Lupo.)* Tell me, shepherd, have you seen the orphan cortège of shadows march past? Perhaps Leticia, in her sparkling dress, was one of them? Didn't her body shine brightly like a piece of good news in the midst of so much dark calamity? Speak without fear, for no one is listening to us. Isn't that right, friends?

*(The courtiers agree.)*

DON LUPO *(Regaining his composure.)* No, I certainly did not see anything, if you can call that obsolete adjective and that harsh epithet "seeing."

AGRIFONTE *(Aside.)* Is he mocking me? Let's find out. *(Out loud.)* Tell me, are you the cruel Wenceslas, that agnostic?

DON LUPO Who do you take me for, in Christ's name!

AGRIFONTE For yourself.

*(Don Lupo is stricken with a fit of violence. His eyes brim with deadly hate. In one move, he unsheathes his miserable sword.)*

DON LUPO Repeat, if you please, those mutilated—indeed, let me tell you once and for all—those cretinous words.

AGRIFONTE I was saying that . . .

*(He can't finish, because Don Lupo, with festering rage, takes his sword in both hands and swings.)*

DON LUPO Take that. And that. And that. But are you still doing fine, my friend?

AGRIFONTE I'm fine. And you?

DON LUPO  Nothing new, thank God. And your presumed family? And Hamlet?

AGRIFONTE  He's coming this way now, sleepless and virginal. Would you like me to introduce you? *(Calling Hamlet.)* Hey, my good man.

HAMLET  *(As if waking from a dream.)* Who calls for me thus? *(He stares at them.)* Speak.

*(Don Lupo and Agrifonte realize that Hamlet knows everything. They are livid with rage and disgust.)*

DON LUPO  We swear we did not know . . .

HAMLET  To have or to hold, that is the rot.

AGRIFONTE  This is too much. *(He goes to the town hall, picks up the document, and returns.)* Hamlet, my friend, your father, the good father who gave you this whole business, just died unexpectedly.

HAMLET  *(Lost, laughing with infinite bitterness.)* Ha, ha, ha . . . My father gave me this whole business. What a business! *J'en pense le plus de mal possible.** 

THE FATHER'S GHOST  *(Appearing.)* Sirs, dinner is served.

*(They all exit. The now vacant landscape is reminiscent of one of those shameless participles that once delighted our ancestors.)*


## Act IV

*(A cemetery—cimenteri in Catalan—choked amid the madrepore of its tombs. It's raining.)*

HAMLET  *(With a fake mustache and beard.)* Come, girls, come to the sweet royal feast. We'll hear the ticktock of bells turn into the beating of hearts. Come, girls, your month of May now wishes to become breasts.

---

*["I couldn't possibly think any worse of it," in French in the Spanish original.—Trans.]

*(Time passes.)*

Maidens, where are you now, maidens. I see your wombs are intact, but on each finger you have a jet of broken veins.

*(Time passes.)*

Women, aren't you tired of giving birth? See how many armies, issued from you, fight upon the earth. And those swords? You have forged them with the beating of your heart. That's why your timid breasts— already vanquished—announce the final sunset.

*(Time passes. A red wire bicycle cuts through the sky. Hamlet takes off his fake mustache and beard and looks youthful and eternal once more. He exclaims:)*

Oh, once they were girls and now they are frail old women, flatulent mothers of all calamity with gray, limp mustaches. What good is the wrinkled skin of your drum? Girl or maiden, woman or old lady, that is your dilemma: thus Boy = Girl; then I say to you that Man is what we wanted to prove.

AGRIFONTE *(Dressed like a gravedigger.)* You were saying, Hamlet, my friend . . .

HAMLET  I was saying, and I stand by it, that the hidalgo's name was Don Rótulo Apodaca.

AGRIFONTE *(Annoyed again.)* He is Apodaca and you'll be Daca.

HAMLET  And if I were . . .

AGRIFONTE  Then . . . well actually, I don't know.

*(A cavalcade stops in front of the castle door. Margarita dismounts from her horse, hurries up the stairs, and enters the cemetery like a madwoman.)*

MARGARITA *(Throwing herself on Hamlet's corpse.)* Oh, impossible, impossible. *(She sobs.)* Poor Hamlet, here he lies dead, taken from me forever, eternally unattainable. *(She sobs.)* Poor Hamlet, so punctual, so good. We could have been so happy, O Agrifonte. But he never understood me; no, he never understood me, and he'll never keep our date. Have you seen him today?

AGRIFONTE *(Lewdly and perversely.)* No. I've been waiting for him myself. And you, Margarita, is your smile just gloomy or are you still unsatisfied?

MARGARITA I want to see Hamlet, my love.

AGRIFONTE *(Grabbing the keys and his hoe.)* Let's go, then.

*(They disappear down a dark street in a loving embrace. Margarita has left her sex behind on the cross above a tomb. Hamlet remains in his hiding place, from which he will have followed, with growing anguish, what we have already related.)*

Scene 2

*(The sea. Agrifonte, the companion, Don Lupo, and Hamlet on a ship. A white procession of dead children begins to filter through the skylight.)*

DON LUPO *(From the top of the foremast, his telescope at the ready, he smells rather than surveys the horizon.)* Hey! All you on board! A small brigantine off starboard.

*(The three friends point their flaccid spyglasses to port. Leticia, smiling, without a crinoline, makes several incredible signs at them.)*

DON LUPO *(From the foremast.)* Do you see her?

HAMLET *(Distantly.)* Yes, I see her.

COMPANION I don't.

AGRIFONTE I don't see her and I don't know her. So until tomorrow, gentlemen. I always retire early. *(He exits.)*

COMPANION Goodbye, Hamlet. Have fun. Oh! I nearly forgot. The cardinal has forgiven you. *(He also exits.)*

HAMLET *(Aside.)* Why are they leaving? Are we all crazy? *(Out loud.)* You, Don Lupo, perhaps the sanest of us all, cure me of my terrible anxiety, tell me if . . .

*(He can't finish his sentence. Horrified, he sees a numismatic dolphin hurl it-*

*self against Don Lupo and pummel him ceaselessly. The latter lets out a folkloric "Ay!")*

HAMLET *(Somberly.)* Alone on the vast sea, with a ship for a coffin. And without the supreme pleasure of gazing upon Leticia, my only love, the lodestar of my life. *(He shudders.)* But what is this? What have my eyes seen? My God, can it be?

*(Finally . . . At that very place, Leticia, the imponderable Leticia, flows into the sea.)*

*(Delirious, trembling with love.)* Leticia, my Leticia. *(He wraps her in his arms.)*

LETICIA  O Hamlet. Kiss me. Finally I'm yours. Take me.

HAMLET  Leticia, Leticia. All mine . . . ?

LETICIA  Yours forever, my love. All yours and his.

HAMLET  You're his too? My gardener's son's? *(Gazing heavenward.)* Thank you, Lord. *(To Leticia.)* Life of my life.

LETICIA  O love!

*(They collapse into each other's arms, their two bodies one. They laugh, cry, spell out their love. Centuries pass like bats. But . . . suddenly Hamlet turns horribly pale, stumbles backwards, and after letting out a terrible incestuous ay! falls mutilated onto the deck.)*

*(What happened?)*

*(Leticia, the longed-for Leticia, she of the tidy breasts, is none other than Hamlet himself—he, the very Hamlet brought into the world by his mother.)*

THE END

*From the Spanish. Written at Hôtel des Terrasses, Paris, July 6, 1927.*

# Guignol

That he may fill our souls with his joy, Cristobica is here among us to-night, and soon his friend Manlleu will make him pirouette from his prism; but pardon us for a moment if first, as if reaching out a hand to guide him here, to help us get to know him and enjoy a cordial camaraderie with him, we spend a little time talking about Guignol.

## I

Guignol is age-old. It would be impossible to say when he was born: he has always been so young, so fresh, that we cannot believe he is ancient, and yet his ancestors are known in the most remote antiquity. In China, perhaps before anywhere else, there existed articulated dolls; the Egyptians, according to some German scholars, also used dolls in processions and religious festivities. The Greeks called them *neurospertas*, and to what extent they might have resembled the more modern string puppets can be surmised, given that already Aristotle and Plato allude to them; the latter has the Athenian, in a dialog with Clinias, make a comparison between man and doll, one moved by his passions, the other by his strings.

If we can only guess at the existence of a true guignol theater among the Greeks, we can be certain that it existed among the Romans. The various types distinguished under the Roman Republic would characterize the protagonists of all of the puppet theaters that were to emerge from the seventeenth century onward in Naples.

Maccus is the Roman Cristóbal. [*Slide projection.*] We see him here with the same bearded face, dark complexion, hooked nose, and narrow forehead. He was a drunk and a glutton, vain and lustful. These vices dominated his character and always led him into misfortune. He was something of a victim of his own karma, which for him was inexorable; the karma of lost prestige for our Cristobica, to whom bad things did not happen inevitably, but because of some innocent, unforeseen circumstance that brings on the catastrophe, always quelled by his club in the best way possible. The slide that you now see shows a Roman Maccus and an anonymous character, perhaps Pappus, found in excavations carried out on Mount Esquilino, Italy.

They are about 2¾ inches tall, in bronze with silver eyes. Maccus was the main character in Atellan theater, and he had four companions. Bucco, the liar, was impertinent and fairly ingenious. This type also exists in today's guignol, where it is generally an anonymous character, wittier and more cunning than Cristobica; he wins over the latter in every dispute, yet in the end is necessarily defeated by the supreme and unappealable argument of Cristobica's club. Pappus, who in the Italian *pulcinella* would be the equivalent of Pantalone, was an avaricious, lewd old man who, despite his mistrust of everyone, always ended up swindled out of his money and his wife. Dossennus, a philosopher and a hunchback, had good common sense; today his type has disappeared among the puppets, but he lives on in the wings—he is Cristóbal's good friend, who talks to him and gives him comradely advice, and who moves him from within. He takes on the importance of the chorus in Greek tragedy by becoming an intermediary between the audience and Cristóbal.

As indicated a moment ago, the profiles of the guignol puppets we know today were refined in the Italian light comedies of seventeenth-century Naples. Surely these were created by Silvio Fiorillo. [*Slide projection: Pulcinella from 1731.*] Just as in our modern fairs and at the entrances to attractions a monkey is exhibited, a charlatan declaims, or a drum is played by a grotesque and gaudy clown, so at that time burlesque performances would be held to draw the public to the show. In the time of Charles d'Anjou, a certain Pablo Pinella gave these performances, and it is possible that the Italian character of these light comedies owes its name to him. The plot was almost always the same: Pulcinella making fun of Cassandrino. [*Slide projection: Pulcinella from 1831.*]

Originally delightful, these puppet comedies later evolved toward a romantic setting, with shadows under the eyes, languidness, faded roses, and sky-blue sighs. Only the rhythmic grace of a Verlaine or the Versaillesque charm of a Watteau has been able to triumph over the cloying, oversentimental degeneration of Pierrot and Colombine. From the Italian Pulcinella came the English Punch and the French Polichinelle.

The origin of puppet theater in France dates to the sixteenth century. It is probably religious: the *marionettes* perhaps derive their name from the Virgin Mary. More certain is that Polichinelle came to France during the reign of Henry IV. [*Slide projection.*] Here was the nearly perfected type that was preserved until 1834. He was accompanied by Pierrot, Arlequin, the Doctor, Cassandrino, and Colombine.

Soon the Brioché brothers, two French puppeteers, brought Polichinelle his greatest fame. One of the two was summoned to Saint-Germain-en-Laye by Louis XVI (1669) to alleviate the boredom of the dauphin's childhood for two months. The life of the last Brioché offers a peculiar profile. He had been a charlatan and a tooth-puller. Many puppeteers started out with odd and itinerant jobs that freed them completely from the bourgeois proletariat, giving them so much independence and liberty that they were able to nourish their spirits with images unattainable in the mediocrity of normal jobs. A good example of this is the life of Laurent Mourguet, also a tooth-puller, to whom we shall return later. Thus we have José Vera, a street musician; Juan de las Viñas, an old beggar; Manlleu, a wild animal trainer, and many more. In literature too, the puppeteer is portrayed as a man who has held absurd jobs, the most famous being Ginesillo de Pasamonte. Brioché also had a trained monkey that Cyrano de Bergerac ran his sword through, punishing its irreverence at having made a gesture regarding his nose.

A century later, Dominique Seraphin, under the reign of Louis XVI, created a small theater for children where he put on shadow plays. He had many anonymous collaborators, to whom he paid twelve livres for each little play. In 1788 his nephew brought the well-known puppets onto the shadow play stage. This evolution continued, reaching a point where the Pupazzi de Lemercier de Veuville even put on a show in the Tuileries before Napoleon III. Fearing that the emperor might be bored by the show, someone asked, "Is he having a good time?" "I think so," came the answer. "He is laughing in a way that is most unusual for him."

As we can see, France is where the puppet theater known to all of us has the most history. Pulcinella is called Guignol there and has acquired French nationality. Thus it was proclaimed by Henry Robert, former president of the bar association in Paris.

France has Guignol: audacious, noisy, viperish, daring, he sometimes flouts good manners—he makes fun of the judge, hits the soldier, clubs or wallops the commissary, drives the landlord to ruin—but at heart he is generous and a good kid. He is very much of this country in which revolutions are made with songs. He has the little mask of Figaro but also that of Cyrano. He is of our careless race, but quick-witted by tradition; his clever turn of phrase makes all be forgiven. An *enfant terrible*, he is nonetheless well loved, and no one has the courage to scold him.

The city of Lyon is home to this charming character. He emerged at the end of the eighteenth century and was of popular origin, the brother of the third estate and of the silk merchants of Lyon. His father's name was Laurent Mourguet. He was something like the Molière of puppet theater, yet he lived in almost complete obscurity. He was the son of a Lyon weaver and a silk worker himself, without any means. He had no skills; he could not even read or write. The upheaval of the Revolution led him to leave his job. Later he became a merchant, then, in 1788, a tooth-puller in public squares. This new occupation set him on the stage of what would soon be his art. Frequenting fairs, he found himself amid the hustle and bustle of the booths and would often see Polichinelle, still at work in France since his arrival under the reign of Henry IV.

In 1804 he put up a small theater in Brotleaux that he named Castelet. He soon began to innovate, modifying the main character, still Polichinelle, but he was not really sure that his changes were wise. Don't be surprised at this timidness, and above all do not think him any less brilliant for it; it is difficult to innovate, and when we venture for the first time onto an unknown path, we take hesitant steps and look for an expert guide to give direction and confidence to our strides. Mourguet got into the habit of discussing his innovations with a good friend who was a cobbler, ingenious and original, called Father Thomas. This habit is completely irreproachable. Molière used to test out his latest comedies on his maidservant. Every time Laurent Mourguet invented something for his Castelet, before confronting the public's judgment he would seek out Thomas's. His approval was manifested in a hearty, frank laugh, crowned with the exclamation: *C'est guignolant!* This good cobbler had his original vocabulary, just as Belarmino, Pérez de Ayala's cobbler, had his. He had as much right to it, too, since both were creators in their own way. Mourguet found the expression funny, and he had his characters say it. The audience enjoyed the new meaning of the word, which soon became a nickname for the one who deserved it. Thus was the puppet christened, and from then on Polichinelle would everywhere be called Guignol.

Now let us see what innovations Mourguet brought to his theater. Of course, he created a new type for the main character. He stylized Polichinelle and made him into a true urban figure. He now dresses like the Lyon silk merchants, in a long frock coat, poor and tattered, and a wig with a braid. His weapon is his cane, and he employs it constantly when he wants to impose his will. Mourguet also increased the number of puppets, basing their characters on people he knew. Madelon, Guignol's wife, was surely inspired by his own wife, and Gnafron, Guignol's constant companion, was a caricature of the cobbler Thomas. He also created a few short tales that were to become typical on the guignol stage. Guignol's disputes with the landlord and his constant battles with the police achieved an ingenious and entertaining expression. Here is a dispute between Guignol and his landlord. Guignol has nine unpaid bills; he and Gnafron are talking.

GNAFRON: Nine bills! You mean you've never paid him anything?

GUIGNOL: Not a thing.

GNAFRON: Embrace me, Guignol, I have always loved you, you are a model tenant. (*M. Ganezou, the landlord, interrupts.*)

GANEZOU: Mr. Guignol, Mr. Guignol!

GUIGNOL (*hiding*): I am not here.

GANEZOU: Then how can you answer?

GUIGNOL: I can't come out. I am mending my pants.

GANEZOU: I need to speak with you. Do you want to come out? I have come to find out when we can settle our account.

GUIGNOL: Our account? If you owe me a few trifles, don't worry, it's not urgent.

GANEZOU: What stories won't you tell to keep me standing this long?

GUIGNOL: Ah, you're right; let's get to bed!

Still later, a new variety of the French Guignol appeared in Paris. The son of Guignol, Gringalet, whom Anatole France said partook of the divine, enriched the existing cast of characters and took his place at center stage. He is brazen and mischievous. He makes fun of gendarmes and hits his father, but all his wrongdoing is easily forgiven because he is so funny. His exploits reflect the superiority of his genius. So it was that in Paris, guignol became essentially a children's show.

In Liège there existed a puppet theater whose Guignol was named Chaucet. He had Polichinelle's great Cyranesque nose. He was familiar, lovable, subtly malicious—a bit disconcerting at base. When he finished his performance, he would approach his admiring audience of children and say, "Who wants to punch me in the nose?" And all would punch him, applauding this Chaucet with the prodigious nose who made them laugh so hard.

In Germany, Guignol is called Johnny Sausage, Hanswurst. He is very insolent and insults the divinity, whom he does not treat very nicely in a play titled *The Fall of Adam*, which was performed in Königsberg in the eighteenth century. In 1737 the poet Gottsched, wanting to purify German theater, burned Hanswurst during the presentation of a tragicomedy that he had had mounted appropriately. But this attack had such negative repercussions that the poet immigrated to Russia, and Hanswurst won all the prestige, taking root in the public's devotion.

Similar to Hanswurst was the Pickle-herring of the Dutch. Kasperle represented the Austrian peasant of the Danube.

The Turkish version was more of a shadow theater than a puppet theater. Karagueuz, the protagonist, personified the devil. Tondon was a malicious maiden; Korards Chodsche, a hunchbacked clown; and Hopa, a civil servant. The Persian Kaectchel-Pelevan was bald, that being his defining characteristic, as the humpback was for Pulcinella.

We finally come to our friend Cristobica. Let's give him our attention and listen carefully to his genealogy, for he is so much our own that we might consider him a grotesque brother to us all. The same unknown origin that makes it difficult to determine the history of the foreign Pulcinellas arises when we try to find the parents of this Spanish offspring, the member of a knavish, exotic race, cynical and quarrelsome. The earliest allusion that hints already at a fertile embryo is found in the thirteenth century. It is a kind of prophesy that announces his coming. The jongleurs of that time recited their romances with different vocal nuances and intonations for each of the characters. Guiraut Riquier, the troubadour from Narbonne who lived for many years in the court of the learned king, was no doubt a sensible man and hardly a friend to frivolity—Oscar Wilde would have immediately said "hardly profound"—for in 1274, in his *Suplicatió al rey de Castela per lo noms dels juglars*, he cursed the inferior artists who carried monkeys and puppets:

Ni cels que fan jogars
simis ni bavastel.

Much later, we find new evidence under the reign of Charles V, who, according to Henry Robert, opened the Spanish border to puppeteers who frequently portrayed great bullfights, a puppetry theme that you can still see on our streets today.

Although the form of the main character was not defined until the eighteenth century, small puppet theaters proliferated, so much so that they come to life in the pages of many novels of local customs and manners. I need not remind you of Master Peter's famous puppet show in *Don Quixote*. The esteem in which these puppeteers were held is shown in the happiness that reigns at the inn when Master Peter arrives with his monkey. I have here Clemencín's notes, which perfectly describe technical details that would be difficult to relate in a better way.*

In Master Peter's puppet show, the puppets moved but did not speak; the narrator spoke for all. On other stages, the same puppets acted and spoke with voices represented by whistles and pipes, without hindering an interpreter offstage who explained what the puppets were doing and saying.

In his article "Puppets," Covarrubias also mentions other small figures that moved by themselves on a table in a way that made them seem animated, and he says these were the invention of Juanelo Turriano, "the great mathematician and a second Archimedes."† This kind of set is no longer in use; there are only remnants of it in the monkeys of the blind men and in Don Cristóbal Polichinela, with the blind man and his guide imitating the voices.

In the seventeenth century, in *La pícara Justina*, we also find several details that give some idea of the state of the puppet theater at that time. Justina relates that among her ancestors, all of lowly status, was a great-grandfather who owned puppets in Seville, "the best dressed," she says, "and the best staged that ever came to town." The size of the stage can be gauged from this phrase: "It was small, no bigger than the distance

---

*[Diego de Clemencín (1765–1834) was a Spanish scholar who annotated *Don Quixote*.—Trans.]

†[Sebastián de Covarrubias y Orozco (1539-1613) was a Spanish lexicographer and author of the famous dictionary *Tesoro de la lengua castellana o española* (1611).—Trans.]

from elbow to hand." It's curious that already in the seventeenth century we find the same stage that is used nowadays by our puppeteers. The affection that the common people had for these presentations is confirmed when Justina says, "It gave so much joy to hear his puppet stories that fruit, chestnut, and nougat sellers would often follow behind him." Nevertheless, not everyone would always be pleased with the show, for Cervantes has one of his characters say that the puppeteers were "vagabonds who treated sacred things indecently." Justina's great-grandfather ended his life in this comical and extraordinary manner: he died bashing his head against a rock, since in his madness he believed himself to be a puppet bull. Surely he would have been better off imagining himself Cristobica's club, for then it would have been the rock that had a rough time.

We find allusions to puppets in many sixteenth- and seventeenth-century works. Let us cite, among others, Cristóbal Suárez de Figueroa and Cosme Gómez de Tejada. The first, in *La Plaza universal de todas ciencias y artes*, appeals for the preservation of puppets, calling them "ministers of noteworthy amusement," and the second, in the *León prodigioso*, describes a long puppet show; yet in descriptions from that era, guignol always has an epic and erudite character that today it has happily lost and that even then was missing in the original shows put on by puppeteers. The grotesque and the ingenious, products of the people, have advantageously replaced the affectation and philosophical nuance of those who wrote about guignol in literature. We prefer the spontaneous guignol of a former lion trainer or a cobbler to the anxious one of a poet or literary writer.

To end this brief genealogy of Don Cristóbal Polichinela, we mention that the last popular genius who cultivated this genre, one suffused with the profound emotion of the streets, was Juan de las Viñas, an old man who could be seen in Madrid some forty years ago. His only stage decor was his cape, held high by a helper who moved the puppets while the old man fine-tuned the various voices and invented new episodes and adventures. Today two puppeteers wander through the streets of

Madrid: Manlleu and José Vera. The first presents a more cultured popular guignol, the other a more barbarous one.

Guignol also exists overseas. In Chile, for example, we find Don Cristóbal married to Doña Clara, whom he brings to her senses from time to time with his club, amid insults and recriminations from Mama Laucha, his mother-in-law. A black character, Federico, also has his part, representing a wide section of the South American public.

All these historical notes allow us to make some observations about the character of today's guignol.


## II

Cristobica is the brother of the people; his every movement exalts in the sunny streets of the city. The joyous democracy of the hubbub there traces a kind of ideal frame around his theater, which merges with the street through that virtue of continuity that Ortega y Gasset once observed as a property of the frame. In light of this theme we can elaborate a few thoughts that all will recall. The theater of Guignol is an essentially popular art form, and in this advantage lies most of its merit. It is so difficult to achieve spontaneously, and with natural freshness, the emotion found in the hearts and gestures of everyone! That is why so few poets have managed to base their songs in the people, and those who succeeded have done so only because the words in their verses came directly from the people, so that the poet's soul was no more than a resonator for the souls of all. Not to make art for the people, but to make art of the people—that is the true path of emotion. The artist who creates this work has no real personality; his profile is blurred in the anonymous outline of the profile of the people. Who could name the author of the most beautiful ballad that travels through the emotions of every villager's soul? The poet Manuel Machado said it best:

Until the people sing them,
ballads are not ballads;

and when the people sing them,
no one knows their author.

Similarly, as already noted, we cannot pinpoint the rise of Guignol. In every country he emerges from the very mass of the people, singled out by his gestures. He always embodies the psychology of his compatriots. Perhaps when he is born he acts out comedies or farces that are not completely of the people, that his manipulator has created based on his memory of this or that great work of theater. But soon enough, by a natural phenomenon of imitation, he assimilates all the popular qualities that turn him into a democratic character. This process imparts the specific differences that distinguish every national Guignol. The Germans, for example, would never accept a southern Guignol. The English Punch is a humorist; the German Hanswurst is petulant and gluttonous; the Belgian Chaucet, is, like the Flemish, a bit naughty but a good person; the Turkish Karagueuz is brazen, sensual, and libidinous.

Our Cristobica, as Manlleu will soon demonstrate on his stage, is an individualist, passionate, obstinate, perhaps a bit too wild, but of course a good fellow, inoffensive and deliciously ingenious. He is also—we cannot omit these two qualities—somewhat irreverent and shameless. He has inherited much, without realizing it perhaps, from the foul-mouthed, funny, and mischievous protagonists of our picaresque novels, and not a little too from the clowns of our classical theater. Moreover, Cristobica has a continuous urge to quarrel and always ends his disputes with a drubbing. We admire in this behavior a healthy energy, a colorful dynamism; Cristobica's rich character deserves our cordial sympathy. Through him we draw close to a healthy happiness with no rhyme or reason, one that clothes our spirits in raiments of light for the celebration within.

He is, above all, a good example for those whose posture is excessively rigid, as they sit on the static benches of their upright and spiritless paths—those poor souls who are too weary under the great weight of their good sense to ever trace that ideal pirouette, so amusing and contented, that manages to free us, bringing us to the point of an ennobling simplicity, concise and pure like the simplicity of the passions in this innocent and childish theater that seems to have the same naked structure as the geometric simplicity of the parallelepiped through which Cristobica peeks out at us. Making the same observation, Anatole France has said, "I would never dare to compose phrases for the illustrious mouths of the actresses of the Comédie Française. I know nothing of such well-plotted intrigues. If I were to write drama, I would write for the marionettes: all of my art would consist of painting the passions, having chosen the simplest ones, and this would be worthless for the Gymnase, the Vaudeville, or the Comédie Française; but it would be perfect for guignol. That is where the passions are dominating and simple."

This whole schematic structure, these simple lines of emotion are obtained because the cast has been reduced to a specific number of characters, who are always the same and familiarly known by all. The passions that rage in each puppet's soul are unique; each character is animated by a passion that defines it and that in turn confronts another passion. Thus, all conflict is sketched out at once in a sure plan. The farce suddenly engages us, and the battle holds us in its sway.

Nevertheless, it must be noted that this internal, emotional simplicity is not without the baroque flavor that the puppet stage imparts. The former is the essential quality, the content; the latter is rather an external characteristic, the form. It is found in the costumes, the gestures, the voices of the puppets: gaudy colors, exaggerated movements, and false cries. Thus Guignol can become, as Henry Robert has said, "a comic caricature of man as we see him, or as we thought we saw him, or as we want to see him."

A great wealth of passions can be embodied in these puppets, capable as they are of adopting a host of attitudes instantaneously; in view of their dynamism, George Sand has said, "With movement, these figures, sketched lightly and painted in rather dark or opaque matte tones, little by little give the appearance of life. They come and go, turn their heads, cross their arms or raise them to the sky or shake them in all directions, giving greetings, throwing punches, hitting the walls in joy or desperation. We begin to forget that they are dolls. We think we see all the emotions drawn in their faces. And this marvel results from the fact that these are not automatons of sorts, devoid of feeling, but rather soft and obedient instruments of human inspiration expressed directly in front of the spectator through the skillful play and varied intentions or reflexes of the fingers."

An abundance of aesthetic ideas wells up at the mere thought of a puppet theater—inspirations for achieving simpler and more reduced forms oriented toward a healthy theater, one in which all the emotional force would rest on the sober simplicity of the scenic elements and on the interior nakedness of the passions. Only in Russian theater, marked by a need to incorporate the emotion of guignol into other shows, has this orientation perhaps been fully realized. Note, for example, its intense importance in *Petrouchka*. From the moment the puppet show appears at the fair, it lives on in the spirit of the whole ballet. "The Good Doctor" in the *Chauve-Souris* is likewise suggested by guignol. A greater scenic complexity distances the puppet show from its primitive structure, but the spirit remains the same. Here is a good example of the way in which elements from puppet theater can be used to create a new artistic show. In the streets guignol must never be touched: no one would dare denature it, just as no one would dare alter a classical romance. But its unadulterated humor can win us over and inspire the creation of a new art that draws on its elements.

Guignol is a fully realized genre: it has its own techniques, namely in the voices, in the way the puppets move, and in the decor. The falsetto voices can be produced with a whistle—a technique called "practice"—or without it, but its use is more frequent. This whistle is none other than a sixteenth-century blowpipe. Through this process a very broad modulation can be attained, and each puppet can speak in the voice that best characterizes him. The "practice" is a rather difficult technique, and it takes long experience to master it. The instrument is held with the tongue against the roof of the mouth. Henry Robert tells us that Charles

Nodier had a puppeteer come to his house to entertain his children. The good academician tried to produce the puppet's nasal tone using the same technique as the performer. When he couldn't do it, the professional made him try again. "I'm afraid I'll swallow it," said Nodier. The puppeteer answered him calmly, "It doesn't matter, nothing would happen to you. I've swallowed that very same piece you have in your mouth more than ten times." Nodier gave up his lesson after that.

The different methods of moving the puppets have led to different types of guignol. The most complicated way is with strings, and from time to time—very rarely now, sad to say—this can still be seen at fair booths. [*Slide projection.*] Each gesture, each position, is dependent on a string: the puppets have delicate movements, and as they walk they glide smoothly, like quiet figures in dreams. This type of guignol allows for a greater number of puppets. [*Slide projection.*] In "The Good Doctor," which we mentioned in speaking of the *Chauve-Souris*, the puppets move only their arms. The same actor who sticks his head out over the puppet's neck, as in those cutouts photographed at fairs, moves its arms while hidden behind it. In this slide we can see the puppets by Madame Forain, whose models were used in the *Chauve-Souris*. Another method is that of our modern-day puppeteers: the index finger, which is the most expressive of all, is inserted into the head of the puppet, and the thumb and the middle finger work the arms. Finally, we have automaton puppets, like those exhibited by Walder and Sanz in variety theaters and in the circus ring.

The guignol puppets can adopt a wide range of personalities. In their gestures we can see portrayed those of any character we might wish to imagine. As elements of fiction, they are rich in suggestive powers.

The stage used in guignol street theater typically has two forms: the one you see here and another consisting of a similar structure, with a window at the front open at the level of the head of the man who sits behind it and operates the puppets.

In listening to these notes, you have seen how guignol is above all a show that is bound to entertain children. It is full, in fact, of a moving childlike happiness, and its passions reach small souls with an intense affectionate vibration. On account of Cristobica's joy, sometimes senseless or absurd and always congested, the spirits of children open to a festival filled with good, pure light. Each puppet in the shrill farce could be the child's friend and his toy, and in it he discovers a hero who is different every time and whom he clothes in all the fantasies he can imagine. The extraordinary variety of scenes, their stirring activity and simple and concrete structure are well defined in the child's intelligence. Above all, the child wants action, dynamic existence, such that at any moment he himself could be a character in the tragicomedy. This possibility, which instantly opens an entire world before him, is the child's satisfaction. Anatole France, taking his little friend Suzanne by the hand, saw this very thing in guignol. Here is how he puts it in a paragraph from *Le Livre de mon ami:* "Yesterday I took Suzanne to the guignol. We both really enjoyed it; it's a theater aimed right at our level of understanding."

It's unthinkable that a moral thesis might grab a child's attention. What entertains him is irreverence and foolish action. He finds emotion not in the outcome but in every moment, and beauty is always revealed to him in the pleasure that moment produces. At times this beauty exerts a prodigious fascination that is only possible in children. Frequently, when he appears shrieking with his club, the bearded Cristóbal scares the smallest children, the ones so little that their nannies have to hold them up so that they can see the show: they grow anxious, start to cry, and do not want to be near Guignol. A few days ago, in Rosales, a little blond young lady was kicking in her nanny's arms and could not be consoled when the devil screamed in front of Cristóbal. Maurice Donnay relates a beautiful gesture: "A guard had been brutally beaten by Guignol and Gringalet; all battered, he was hanging from the edge of the stage. 'Come to my rescue, dear children!' he shouted. Then a little girl, blushing and trembling, timidly approached and picked the beaten policeman back up."

And now, friends, it is Guignol who will speak to you. From this little stage, pure emotion, got up grotesquely and speaking in falsetto, will greet the friendly, joyful soul that we always carry within us. We wish to say, "Here is Master Manlleu; a wonderful evening is upon us."

All that's missing for Guignol to be in his element is the baroque commotion of a small plaza filled with children and the Sunday sunshine. Let's make up for it with our own goodwill and open our hearts, bringing them fresh air and rejuvenating them with Cristóbal's childish escapades.

*From a lecture in Spanish. N.d.*

ON CINEMA

# A Night at the Studio des Ursulines

Tonight's program begins with a promise of ten minutes of prewar cinema. The lights go down.

Spiritism? Rusty shadows glow anew in a second existence. Whirlwind of old memories. Czar Nicholas II advances, surrounded by showy Orthodox priests. How pathetic is the smile he flashes as he passes before the lens! Surely one of the Russians in the theater will have cried upon seeing that face spread into a smile from beyond the grave. Now a primitive Renault, which M. Poincaré steps out of, makes us appreciate that much more the beauty of the latest-model Packard or Issota-Francini. Then comes the *tango milonga*. The professor's mustache is wider than his partner's waist. With all the solemnity in the world, the two abandon themselves to the most ridiculous movements, and the audience can't stop laughing until the end of the reel, because it immediately moves on to fashion. A natural history course on hats. The models move like hens. From the front, the back, the sides, they engage in a competition of collars, lace, silks, percales. We find ourselves serious again. We even muse that our own epoch is a paragon of taste . . . and of simplicity. By dint of complexity, if you will. These prewar newsreels are the epilogue to the contemporary age. And even if this ending is fiction, it suffocates us.

The grotesque culminates in the projection of an early movie drama. Photographed theater. The stationary lens limits itself to reproduction. Its only virtue is silence: fortunately, we don't hear the words that accompany the action. In their place, no doubt, the actors gesticulate wildly, in the midst of abject scenery. Three or four knife thrusts from the bearded protagonist put an end to the film and to our laughter.

The evolution of cinema has been rapid—and alarming. It would seem—if we put aside the infinite possibilities of three-dimensional color—to have reached if not the end then at least the limits of its technical evolution. That being so, in a few years, won't the film that now seems exceptional make us smile in the same way? This is one of the most serious objections that can be raised against cinema. If the work of art withstands the passing of centuries, its pristine beauty kept always whole and fresh, why is film, a victim of time, subject to such deplorable senility? Certainly, early cinema hadn't found its own language, its own particular means of expression. None of the four main pillars that support the great temple of Cinematics had been constructed—neither the detached shot, nor camera angles, nor lighting, nor editing and composition, the strongest and most definitive support. A film, like a play, unfolds in space and time. But whereas space and time are fixed forever in film, without any possible evolution, in theater the styles and tastes of the day introduce appropriate variations—hence, the stage adaptation. Thus, the tastes of each epoch, powerless before the definitive quality of film, will be the strongest depreciator of its aesthetic value.

It has been said that by stylizing costumes, architecture, etc., we may attenuate such a tragic end. But won't the entire ensemble, perhaps the procedure itself, also appear dated? We must return to this extremely important question.

Coordinations and combinations of luminous rays taken from epoch $x$ to another epoch $x$ yield the *avant-guerre* film. Now Cavalcanti has come along to demonstrate that when such rays are taken to epoch $x + 10$ years, we get the *avant-garde* film, the purest expression of the present age.

We first knew Alberto Cavalcanti as the art director of *Feu Mathias Pascal*. Then, as a filmmaker, he directed a screenplay by Louis Deluc, *Le Train sans yeux*. Today he has proven to be a great hope of French cinema, figuring among its most youthful and sensitive practitioners.

*Rien que les heures:* Nothing but the hours. No loves, no hatreds, no denouement with a final kiss. The hour hand's blind revolution twenty-four times a day. The city's ideal day's run toward the future.

Cavalcanti begins by showing us Paris as seen by the most fashionable painters of the rue de la Boétie. Then the city seen through the lens. Main character: a clock.

Day breaks. A yawn and a blind being raised. The first delicate wisps of morning smoke in the chimneys. The sepulchral doors of a metro station open halfway: the daily resurrections are about to begin. Baskets of fruits and vegetables. In a street filmed from above, an old woman drags along in her tatters—in her drunkenness or her pain? Goods for sale. Cars rolling by. The crescendo of morning. Wheels, pulleys: work and activity in full swing. Midday. A laborer sleeps in the bright sun of one o'clock. Insinuated velocities. Early edition newspapers and afternoon shadows. The feet of a worker leaving the job rise on tiptoes so that lips may offer a kiss. The factory gears slow down. Someone is having dinner. A lighted sign: Hotel. A ruffian. Accordion and *bal musette*. A courtesan and an American sailor, on steep streets, like foals. Love and pricing. A crime. The old woman—a strange and impressive leitmotiv—concludes her pilgrimage at the Seine, its waters sparkling with the first light of day. The clock is ready to start over again. What for? The film ends.

This is among the most fully realized of the so-called scriptless films. "Visual" music, the two rhythms of the cinema set out to find the necessary link between the images. Subjective cinema. The viewer must draw on an acquired cinematographic sensibility and education. If someone dared to project this reel before a nonspecialized audience, the insults accompanying it would be something to hear. The anger would be proportionate to the inability to understand.

For lack of space, we cannot elaborate what has merely been insinuated here.

The last film of the repertory is *Greed* by Erich von Stroheim. He alone merits a more extensive treatment than can be given in the present article. We can only lightly sketch out here a few of his most remarkable qualities.

*Greed* is the most unusual, daring, and brilliant film the cinema has yet produced. Upon seeing it, no one can remain indifferent: some may judge it an exemplary film, others may think the director sought to ridicule the rules and imperatives of filmmaking and even of his epoch. But Stroheim would not have worked on it for years just to scoff. He shot more than 325,000 feet of film, of which he wished to keep more than 130,000. An editing specialist had to be brought in to reduce it to its current 9,500-plus feet. It is said that Stroheim kicked and screamed like a child. For several months he suffered from this amputation as if it had been of one of his own limbs.

With the most extreme naturalism, he presents us with abject types, repulsive scenes in which primal and base passions find their most completely realized form. Such mastery in the visualization of all that is most base, ugly, vile, and corrupt in men at once disgusts us and fills us with admiration. He displays an absolute disdain for, or at least indifference to, cinematic tricks, but a grand exaltation in lighting. There is no star, but there are characters that seem sculpted in granite. This new Stroheimian expression has instantly placed itself on a par with Zolaesque values. Naturalism does not interest us in literature or in cinema. Nevertheless, Stroheim's film is magnificent—revoltingly magnificent.

*From the Spanish. Published in* Gaceta literaria, *no. 2, January 15, 1927.*

# *Metropolis*

*Metropolis* is not just one film. *Metropolis* is two films joined at the hip, each with divergent spiritual necessities that are extremely antagonistic. Those who look to cinema as a discreet storyteller will be deeply disappointed with *Metropolis*. What it gives us in the way of story is trivial, turgid, pedantic, and imbued with a stale romanticism. But if we prefer the plastic photographic nature of film to story line, then *Metropolis* will surpass all expectations; it will astonish us like the most marvelous book of images ever composed. It consists, then, of two opposing elements, keepers of the same sign in the zones of our sensibility. The first, which we might call purely lyrical, is excellent; the other, anecdotal or human, ends up being irritating. Both, simultaneously and successively, make up the latest creation of Fritz Lang. This isn't the first time we have witnessed such a disconcerting dualism in Lang's work. For example, interpolated in the ineffable poem *Der müde Tod* are some disastrous scenes of refined bad taste. Since Lang held the role of accomplice, we must denounce his wife, the screenwriter Thea von Harbou, as the presumed author of those eclectic experiments and that dangerous syncretism.

A film, like a cathedral, ought to be anonymous. People of all classes, artists of all types took part in raising this monstrous cathedral of modern cinema — all the industries, all the engineers, the crowds, the actors, the screenwriters, the ace German cameraman Karl Freund, along with a host of colleagues, sculptors all, including Ruttmann, the creator of absolute cinema.* Chief among these architects is Otto Hunte; to him and to Ruttmann, in fact, we owe the most fully realized visualizations in *Metropolis*.† It is as if the set designer—the last vestige of all that the theater bequeathed to cinema—barely makes an appearance here. We sense his presence only in the worst of *Metropolis*, in the pompously named "eternal gardens," done in a raving baroque style of unheard-of bad taste. Henceforth the architect will replace the decorator for good. Film will be the faithful interpreter of the most daring dreams of Architecture.

The clock in *Metropolis* marks only the ten hours of the workday, and the entire city moves to that double-time meter. The free men of Metropolis tyrannize the slaves, the Nibelungs of the city, who work in an eternal electric day in the depths of the earth. All that is missing in the simple mechanism of the Republic is the heart, the emotion capable of uniting such bitter enemies. And in the denouement, we see the director of Metropolis's son (the heart) unite his father (the brain) and the general foreman (the hands) in a fraternal embrace. Mix these symbolic ingredients with a good dose of terrifying scenes and exaggerated, theatrical acting, shake well, and you have the plot of *Metropolis*.

But on the other hand . . . What an exalting symphony of movement! How the machines sing in the midst of wonderful transparencies, crowned by triumphal arches of electrical discharge! All the crystal in the world is romantically shattered into reflections that come to dwell on the modern canon of the screen. Each powerful flash of steel, the rhythmic succession of wheels, pistons, and unknown mechanical forms, is a marvelous ode, a new poetry for our eyes. Physics and Chemistry are

*[Karl Freund (1890–1969) was the director of photography for *Metropolis*. Walter Ruttmann (1887–1941) was an architect and painter who experimented with abstract films after World War I, before turning to documentary.—Trans.]

†[Although he collaborated with Freund on the influential documentary *Berlin: Symphony of a Big City*, which was also made in 1927, Ruttmann is not known to have worked directly on *Metropolis*. Otto Hunte was the art director for several of Lang's films, including *Metropolis*.—Trans.]

miraculously transformed into Rhythm. Not a single moment of ecstasy. Even the intertitles, whether ascending or descending, wandering about the screen, melting into light or dissolving into darkness, join the general movement: they too become images.

In our view, the film's main flaw lies in its failure to follow the idea forged by Eisenstein in *Potemkin*, that of presenting us with a single actor—but one full of novelty, of possibilities: the crowd. The subject of *Metropolis* would have lent itself to that. Instead, we have to endure a series of characters, filled with vulgar and arbitrary passions, fraught with a symbolism by no means appropriate for them. That is not to say that there are no crowds in *Metropolis*, but the crowds seem to serve a decorative role, that of a gigantic "ballet"; they seek more to enchant us with their admirable and balanced movements than to let us understand their souls, their precise obedience to more human, more objective motives. Even so, there are moments—Babel, the workers' revolution, the final persecution of the android—in which both extremes are admirably realized.

Otto Hunte devastates us with his colossal vision of the city in the year 2000. It may be mistaken, even outmoded with respect to the most recent theorizations about the city of the future, but from a photographic point of view, its emotive force and original, surprising beauty are undeniable. It is of such technical perfection that even under prolonged examination, the architectural underpinnings cannot be detected for even an instant.

The making of *Metropolis* cost 10 million gold marks and required the participation, including actors and extras, of some 40,000 people. The present length of the film is more than 16,000 feet, but altogether nearly 6.5 million feet were shot. Tickets for the premiere in Berlin cost 80 gold marks. Doesn't it seem demoralizing that despite such extraordinary resources, the resulting work is no paragon of perfection? In comparing *Metropolis* and *Napoléon*, the two greatest films that modern cinema has created, with others far more humble, yet also purer and more perfect, we may draw the useful conclusion that money is not the most essential ingredient in a modern cinematic production. Compare *Rien que les heures*,* which cost only 35,000 francs, with *Metropolis*. Sensitivity first; intelligence first; and everything else, including money, comes after.

*From the Spanish. Published in* Gaceta literaria, *no. 9, May 1, 1927.*

*[The 1926 documentary by Alberto Cavalcanti (1897–1982), about which Buñuel writes in "A Night at the Studio des Ursulines."—Trans.]

# Fred Niblo's *Camille*

Forgotten in a corner of the literary attic, it could no longer manage to move even the humblest shopgirl. It seemed strange that the young and miracle-working hands of cinema had not brought this corpse—like so many others—back to life. Before anyone could beat him to it, Fred Niblo, the daring creator of *Ben Hur*, set out, camera in tow, for the garden of love, where Mademoiselle Gautier makes her bouquets of camellias. A treacherous journey, it meant venturing into zones diametrically opposed to our sensibilities. A daring journey, it meant marching through hostile territory, well guarded and nearly inaccessible to the lens. But Niblo, with the grace of a poet or a magician, has breathed into Dumas's faltering novel an emotion and vigor it never knew. And here we are now, reacting a bit like shopgirls before this film. Doesn't something similar happen when we watch the latest Chaplin productions, with their mawkish romanticism? (Remember the Christmas Eve scene in *The Gold Rush*. In that regard, Buster Keaton is superior. Such shortcomings have led André Suarès, the great enemy of the seventh art, to speak of the "ignoble heart of Charlie Chaplin.") From a purely cinematic point of view, this might have seemed the film's only appreciable defect. But nonetheless, we dare to assert that Fred Niblo's work is among the most perfect ever made for the screen. The curious thing is that the filmmaker follows the original story, in all its details, from beginning to end.

Further proof of what we have asserted, namely, of the perfect maturity that cinematographic methods are coming to achieve, is the nuance and ennoblement brought to Dumas's work through its transposition to film. Nowadays cinema could not have more disdain for the subject.

Here we see a tendency opposite to that found in fine arts and literature. A "cine-drama," if wisely directed and fully realized, is in the end more novel, more unusual than one of the so-called "visual symphony" films. For in the former—such as the admirable cine-dramatic trilogy formed by *Lady Windermere's Fan*, *The Merry Widow*, and *Camille**— very serious difficulties must be overcome in order to provoke an emotion that is, above all else, specifically cinematic, whether because of the triviality of the theme, the paucity of action, or the difficulty of making visual those elements that are mediocre or too literary. The suggestive power of the image tears us from our seats and throws us in with the characters on the screen. We feel that these phantoms have souls that seem very familiar to us; we come to recognize our own soul in the pair of eyes that look back at us from a close-up. And if we really feel moved, it is because the filmmaker was moved first. *Si vis me flere . . .* This, apart from the plastic and purely visual challenges, is one of the great difficulties of cine-drama.

By contrast, in a musical, the filmmaker relies on qualities essential to cinema even more than upon his own strengths, to the point that the medium becomes far superior to the artist, dominating him and imposing its own logic. More than a conscious creation, his work then seems a simple play on lighting and objects. From the lens, not from the filmmaker, emanates the almost hypnotic power of the image in motion, of its slowed or accelerated rhythms, of its ability to surprise; through editing, our vision moves as swiftly as thought, from the star to the Bugatti, from the landscape to the doorbell, from the tree to the woman's face sculpted in light. Anyone blessed with a particular sensibility could, if he wished, make something similar to Madame Dulac's endeavors,[†]

*[*Lady Windermere's Fan* (1925) was directed by Ernst Lubitsch; *The Merry Widow* (1925) by Erich von Stroheim.—Trans.]

†[Germaine Dulac (Charlotte Elisabeth Germaine Saisset-Schneider; 1882–1942) was a French director in the twenties.—Trans.]

whereas no one but the true artists of silence would be able to construct a film like *Camille*.

Today cinema has at its disposal an almost perfect language of signs. Tomorrow—we await its Messiah—it will have its own ideas. For now, it is dedicated to narrating what has already been told and retold—adaptations; nevertheless, we cannot deny its originality, its personality, its beauty. The fine arts are as old as humanity. The fine industry that is cinema has no need to conform to laws that were forged over many centuries. It will create its own history and its own aesthetics. For now, it wants no more than to add to the half-dozen works on which it rests.

With great discretion and artistry, Fred Niblo has avoided all that was visually ugly in the time of Marguerite Gautier. He stylizes the interiors in perfect taste. The costumes, though contemporary, have a subtly evocative feel. Everything is imbued with the feeling and character of the period, alive and beating like a heart.

Apparent even in the most insignificant detail is the desire to compose the visual field. Without this, no good film is possible; it is the great concern of contemporary filmmakers. Psychologically as well as materially, in the plastic photographic space, Niblo composes the interiors, the medium close-ups, the still lifes—*dans le cinéma il n'y a pas de nature morte. Les objets ont des attitudes.** The emotion of silver and silk, of camellias like tears, of young lips and hands. An exquisite, veiled emotion like a distant memory. For the entire film is a pure and ineffable memory, and so it begins, upon being lived again by one of its characters: Armand, looking at the painting of Marguerite. The effects are perfectly realized, thanks to the continuous use of gauze and the soft-focus lens in medium close-ups. In wide shots the photography is sharp, and it stands out among the best.

The play of wide shots, so economical and restrained, never becomes

*["There is no such thing as still life in cinema. Objects have attitudes." Buñuel is quoting Jean Epstein, the avant-garde theorist and filmmaker with whom he worked as assistant director on *La Chute de la maison Usher* (1928). —Trans.]

tiresome. Frequently combined with panoramas, they bring us, as if on a tray, in slow rhythms, even the most hidden desires of the characters. Marguerite and Armand first fall in love in silence and in light; later their love becomes emotional and discreet. We point out the magisterial use of dissolves in the final scenes in the country house. Those in the game room are more commonplace, and therefore less interesting.

It is here that Constance Talmadge has left us with her most delicate impression.* She and all the actors do not portray their roles; they live them. "It seemed to us that they were taking dictation from life, unlike those in the theater, who simply take up what has already been dictated," as Ramón Gómez de la Serna would have said. In the depths of their pupils—close-up—motives lurk constantly. Their feelings are translated into movements, which are then combined, multiplied, and analyzed by the editing. Let's not forget that this is the same man who made the chariot race in *Ben-Hur*, a paradigm of editing.

The film will come to you mutilated, chopped up with intertitles, accompanied intermittently by a *pasodoble* or *La Traviata*. They'll give you almost a different film. But go, if you can, with good intentions and with cotton in your ears, to take in *Camille* by Fred Niblo.

*From the Spanish. Published in* Gaceta literaria, *no. 24, December 15, 1927.*

---

*[The role was in fact played by Norma Talmadge, Constance Talmadge's older sister. Both were well known at the time.—Trans.]

# Abel Gance's *Napoléon*

It seems to me that the art of cinema is inherent to the people of the North, and that we Latins, laden with tradition, mysticism, culture, ecstasy—sensitive receivers of other forms of art—are incapable of assimilating that of motion pictures. Each one of our attempts underscores the superiority of the people of the New World over us.

American films in general are often criticized as trivial. But any one of them, even the most modest, always has a primitive ingenuity, a comprehensive photographic charm, an absolutely cinematic rhythm.

The Americans have opened our eyes to the essence of drama—drama itself is only secondary—and when they discover something new, they never misuse it. They don't overdo it, for their way of being always drives them further on.

It is indisputable that they possess a much greater feel for cinema than we do.

It is true that many among the social elite have a certain prejudice against the seventh art. But it is just as true that, carried along by the current of the times, they would be willing to embrace any noble attempt. For that to happen, the right film would have to be created to introduce them to the limitless possibilities of cinema. Perhaps out of faith in the most esteemed critics' hype, the unbelieving have gone to see *Napoléon*, and what have they deduced?

Gentlemen, we say to them, this is not cinema. This does cinema an injustice. You're better off going to see *L'Ingénue*, an American film about a lovestruck equestrienne that ends with a discreet kiss; at least it's light, fresh, full of rhythmic images, fashioned in flashes of truly cinematic intuition.

*From the French. Published in* Cahiers d'art, *no. 3, 1927.*

# Victor Fleming's
## *The Way of All Flesh*

Technical ability is a necessary quality in a film, as in all other works of art—indeed, even in an industrial product. But it mustn't be thought that this quality determines the merit of a film. There are other qualities in a film that can be more interesting than technical skill. Of course, viewers never bother to analyze the technical means that make a film; most of the time they ask only that the film touch their emotions. But emotion must not be confused with sentimentality. Devoid of authentic emotion, Victor Fleming's film is, ultimately, a counterfeit. Although technically excellent, this film shares with many others the distinction of appealing more to our tear glands than to our sensibilities. One could hear the tears falling on the theater floor. Everyone was exposed deep down as a crybaby at the showing of *The Way of All Flesh*.

Why not institute the practice of subjecting films, before showing them to the public, to minute inspection under a microscope? That would be the instrument best suited to examining them. Had it been put to such use, we would certainly have discovered that Fleming's cinedrama was crawling with melodramatic germs, completely infected with sentimental typhus mixed with romantic and naturalistic bacteria.

We had been under the impression that our time and its cinema had completely rid themselves of such an anachronistic epidemic. But venom must be fought with venom, and cinema with cinema.

*From the French. Published in* Cahiers d'art, *no. 10, 1927.*

# Buster Keaton's *College*

Here is Buster Keaton with his latest film, the wonderful *College*. Asepsis. Disinfection. Freed from tradition, our gaze revels in the juvenile, tempered world of Buster, the great specialist in fighting sentimental infections of all kinds. The film is as beautiful as a bathroom, as vital as a Hispano-Suiza. Buster never tries to make us cry, for he knows that cheap tears are outdated. He is not, however, a clown who makes us roar with laughter. Not for a minute do we stop smiling, not at him but at ourselves—smiling at health and Olympian force.

In cinema, we always contrast Keaton's monotonous expression with the infinitesimal variations of a Jannings.* Filmmakers overdo it with Jannings, multiplying his slightest facial contractions to the $n^{th}$ degree. For him, suffering is a prism cut into a hundred facets. That's why he's capable of acting in a close-up from 150 feet, and if one were to ask even more of him, he'd manage to show us how an entire film could be made of nothing but his face, a film that might be called *Jannings's Expression; or the many combinations of* M *wrinkles raised by the power of* n *to* n.

Buster Keaton's expressions are as modest as, for example, a bottle's; the dance floor of his pupils is round and clear, but there his aseptic spirit does pirouettes. The bottle and Buster's face have infinite points of view.

*[Emil Jannings (1884–1950), Swiss-born actor who worked briefly in Hollywood at the end of the silent era, won an Oscar for his role in *The Way of All Flesh* in 1927.—Trans.]

Few are those who know how to accomplish their mission in the rhythmic, architectural workings of a film. It is the editing—film's golden key—that combines, comments on, and unifies all these elements. Can greater cinematic virtue be reached? Some have wanted to believe in the inferiority of Keaton as the "anti-virtuoso" in comparison with Chaplin, considering this a handicap, a sort of stigma, whereas we consider it a virtue that Keaton achieves comic effect though direct harmony with the tools, situations, and other means of production. Keaton is loaded with humanity—but a recent and wholly original humanity; a fashionable humanity, if you will.

Much has been said about technique in films like *Metropolis* and *Napoléon*. No one ever talks about technique in films like *College*, and that is because the technical achievements are so indissolubly mixed with other elements that we aren't even aware of them, just as we don't give thought to the strength ratings of the building materials for a house we are living in. The super-films serve as a lesson to technicians; Keaton's films give lessons to reality itself, with or without the techniques of reality.

The Jannings School: European style: sentimentalism, antiquated notions about art and literature, tradition, etc. John Barrymore, Conrad Veidt, Ivan Mozhukhin, etc.

The Buster Keaton School: American style: vitality, a cinematic essence, a shortage of culture, and fledgling traditions: Monte Blue, Laura La Plante, Bebe Daniels, Tom Moore, Menjou, Harry Langdon, etc.

*From the French. Published in* Cahiers d'art, *no. 10, 1927.*

# Variations on
# Adolphe Menjou's Mustache

Of all the phantasms of flesh and blood on the screen, Menjou would seem to be the one whose private life most closely resembled that quintessential reflection of his life called *film*. Observing him in whichever of those realities, we see in Menjou himself the most extraordinary Menjou that art, literature, or cinema could offer. In a word, Menjou was the most Menjou of all Menjous. And for this sole reason, for having created this type so completely, one lacking the literary baggage of Don Juan but much more photogenic, we were bursting with admiration for him. Who doesn't know, moreover, that just as the sirens have their song, so his great Menjouesque powers radiate from his mustache, that brilliant mustache of the movies?

It is often said that the eyes are windows into the soul. A mustache like his can be as well. As he leans so often in close-ups above our heads, what can his eyes tell us that his mustache hasn't already said? A trivial gesture or an almost imperceptible smile acquires, beneath the magic shadow of the mustache, an extraordinary expressiveness; a page of Proust brought to life on the upper lip; a silent but nevertheless comprehensive lesson in irony. Had he not guarded against it, "copyrighting" his mustache, irony would have become standardized, within reach of the most humble of faces.

In the display windows of the future, Menjou's mustache, which embodies the cinema of his time, will replace Napoléon's insufferable and inexpressive hat.

We have seen it, in the close-up of a kiss, settle like a strange summer insect onto lips as sensitive as mimosas and devour them whole, a coleopteran of love. We have seen his smile, from the ambush of his mustache, break through like a sleek, agile tiger and land on its prey, holding his partner's glances forever in its sway.

The last survey concerning Menjou's mustache undertaken among female movie stars in New York was unanimous; they all said the same thing: "His mustache is perhaps the only one that isn't scratchy during a kiss. On the contrary, it produces a delicious, shameful tickle, much prized by all of us."

But Adolphe Menjou's trip to Paris was enough to fill us with confusion. Not because, as he himself declared, he likes Beltrán Massés's painting, which is as good as saying he doesn't care for painting.* The sensibilities and attentions of a "contemporary" man can be directed toward a thousand other things besides painting: he can have exquisite taste without necessarily having to resort to the old platitudes of the arts, and Menjou has shown himself in nearly all his films to be a man of today, with a refined and original temperament; remember, among other things, his stupendous axiom as Monsieur Albert, so representative of his kind: "To make a salad, what matters least are the ingredients, but genius is indispensable."

Neither was our disillusionment caused by what in an another, more vulgar, man might have signaled cretinism or a crass obsession. Adolphe Menjou owns 372 ties, plus one-fourth of a tie still being knitted by the loving fingers of his fiancée, Miss Kathryn Carver.

The intolerable thing about Menjou, what we refuse to believe as if it were a moral impossibility, is that his mustache, his exceptional mustache, is not black, as we all thought, but reddish, the color of saffron, impudently earthy.

*[Federico Beltrán Massés (1885–1949) was a Spanish portrait painter. —Trans.]

"Like the callused hands of the laborer, my mustache does me honor, once black but now bleached by the sweat of my brow beneath the African sun of the spotlights," the accused has said.

But that excuse isn't good enough. If his mustache isn't black, it is as if he didn't have one at all, and without that positive, defining feature of his personality, Menjou could be anyone—anyone but Menjou.

Adolphe Menjou was a modest man, a small-time stage author. Menjou was a poor, clean-shaven man. One day he decided to grow a mustache; all great inventions are the result of chance. On another occasion, in the presence of Chaplin, he thought he'd light a cigarette, and from that moment his great movie career began. For a gesture so trivial, so insignificant, yet so difficult to accomplish acquires astounding proportions on the screen, and that is what a man like Chaplin could not fail to see. No melodramatic gestures; no expressions à la Jannings; no stereotypical fright or surprise—it's enough to know how to raise an eyebrow at the right time and with the right rhythm; the masks of classical theater lower their eyes in shame at the prodigious expressiveness of a Menjou when he exhales that first puff of smoke. Seeing the way he opens an umbrella or hails a taxi, we venture to point out to the crowds the person most gifted for film acting. A movie actor is born, not made. A film, when all is said and done, is composed of segments, a remnant of poses which, taken as such, separately and arbitrarily, are utterly banal, divested of logical meaning, of psychology, of literary transcendence. In literature, a lion or an eagle can represent many things, but on the screen they are only two animals and nothing else, even if for Abel Gance they might symbolize ferocity, courage, or imperialism. That is why so many intelligent people, so many pitiful "art aficionados" are mistaken when they denounce the superficiality of American cinema, without considering that it was the first to realize that the great cinematic truths have no common denominator with those of literature and the theater. Why do they keep calling for metaphysics in cinema and failing to recognize that in a well-made film, the act of opening a door or seeing a hand—

an enormous monster—pick up an object can encompass an authentic and novel beauty? It's always the same scenario that the Americans give us, and it's the one that always seems newest. A wonderful miracle of loaves and fishes! All cinematic value resides in the process, the form; and today this can be held as a fundamental truth, hardly exclusive to cinema.

*From the Spanish. Published in* Gaceta literaria, *no. 35, June 1, 1928. (A shorter version, "Variations on Menjou," had appeared in French in* Cahiers d'art *in 1927.)*

# News from Hollywood

We have spoken with Menjou, who flatly denies an adulterous relationship with his delightful friend Greta Nissen.

"Nevertheless, it's said that you . . ."

Menjou smiles enigmatically. From his jacket he takes out a magnificent gold cigarette case, a gift of the former Kaiser. He opens it and offers it to us filled with mustaches. We take one, thanking him cordially, but still we insist: "They say they saw you . . ."

Menjou has a sincere expression of surprise:

"They saw me; well, who knows? It's quite possible. I've been very absentminded lately."

The other day there was a scandal in Coolidge's Bar, the most frequented bar in Hollywood, when Clara Bow suffered a strange attack in which she suddenly began shouting out for her mother. Everyone stood up, horrified at such effrontery, and there were even a few, including Douglas Fairbanks, who called it "shocking." For two hours, she went on shouting for the woman who brought her into this world, without so much as a thought for her progenitor, and that's what they couldn't forgive her. As a result of this event she was released from Metro, and thirty-two stars immediately asked for their own release, in solidarity with her and with their respective mothers.

Many alarmed readers have written us to make sure of which toothpaste Mary Pickford uses. Don't panic; it was nothing. What happened was that when she couldn't find the one she usually uses at the store, she found herself obliged to buy a tube of a brand called Sot. But as of yesterday, the kind actress has gone back to her usual paste. Admirers of the graceful Mary are satisfied.

Beltrán Massés has finished his portrait of John Gilbert. It is almost better than a photograph, and numerous guests have gone so far as to confuse it with the original and even offer it a cigarette. As a curious detail, we are told that the costume, inspired by the well-known one of England's Henry VIII, is encrusted with real diamonds worth ten thousand dollars. Yesterday John Gilbert organized a reception in honor of the illustrious painter, a worthy successor to Velázquez, attended by Mr. Nicholson, a professor of art at the University of Pennsylvania. He was asked his opinion of the portrait. After reflecting for a moment, he replied: "A magnificent portrait! It looks as if it's going to speak."

That statement gave rise to much discussion, since there are rumors that Mr. Nicholson is preparing a new apparatus that will soon make it possible to converse with paintings in museums.

Jannings's dad was not named Emil but rather Andrew. We have sent telegrams to everyone announcing the news.

Rumor has it that the minister of state education is going to ban all types of cinematographic information and even, it is said, all magazines devoted to the seventh art. It seems the minister has called such material pornographic, accusing it of debasing public taste, nourishing the idiotic banality of the admirers, male and female, of the stars, and continually assaulting the intelligence of the masses. He has imposed stiff fines on important newspapers because, according to him, given the seriousness of which they boasted, it was immoral for them to feature such vile movie pages. In corroboration of this news, we learned yesterday that Baltasar Fernández has been placed under house arrest. We vigorously object to these draconian measures and encourage all noninitiates to go out and read any professional movie magazine or the movie pages of any big city newspaper. The reader will be the judge of the injustice of the minister's actions.

*From the Spanish. Published in* Gaceta literaria, *no. 43, October 1, 1928.*

# Our Poets and the Cinema

There is much talk about the future of cinema. But there are still well-meaning people who discuss the future of the theater. We have transcribed below a paragraph from one of these discourses, and we give our word of honor that we did not make it up, that it is neither a caricature nor a malicious parody of any of those delightful apologists; that would be too extreme a revenge. For the record, this paragraph comes from an article by Antonio Machado, titled, alas, "On the Future of the Theater." It reads:

> Action, in fact, has been almost completely expelled from the stage and relegated to the screen, where it reaches its maximum expression and—let us also say—its reduction to the absurd, to a purely kinetic inanity. There we see clearly that action without words, that is to say, without an expression of consciousness, is nothing but movement, and that movement, aesthetically speaking, is nothing. It's not even an expression of life, since that which is living can be moved or change places in the same way as something inert. The cinema has shown us that a man who enters through a chimney, leaves by a balcony, and then plunges into a pool has about as much interest for us as a ball bouncing off the sides of a billiard table.

How many of us weren't thinking the same thing when, around the year of Our Lord 1908, our parents took us by the hand to the movies to see the unforgettable Toribio enter through a chimney, leave by a balcony, and then jump into a pool! Antonio Machado has taken us back to the carefree, lyrical time of "Mommy, take me to the movies. . . ." But unfortunately, those days are long gone. He should go to the cinema today, then give us his opinion. Here are two films we heartily recommend to him: *The Broken Coin*, with Lucille Love and Count Hugo, and, better still, *The Fatal Kiss*, by Francesca Bertini.

*From the Spanish. Published in* Gaceta literaria, *no. 43, October 1, 1928.*

# Carl Dreyer's *The Passion of Joan of Arc*

Surely this is the freshest, most interesting film in the current motion picture season. Based on an original screenplay by Joseph Delteil, it begins at the moment when Joan appears before her judges, and it ends at the stake.

In this film constructed of close-ups, the director rarely, in fact almost never, employs a general view or even shows the foreground. Each close-up is composed with such care and artistry that these often become paintings without ever ceasing to be shots—ones of exceptional, violently foreshortened angles, the camera almost always off-level.

Not a single actor wears makeup; the sorrowful geography of their faces—their pores like pits—sets this life of flesh and blood into relief. At times the entire screen is filled with the white wall of a cell, and in a corner, the vindictive forehead of a friar—only his forehead. We can anticipate his outbursts with meteorological precision. Noses, eyes, lips that explode like bombs; tonsures, forefingers brandished against the innocent breast of the Maid of Orleans. She answers or cries, or while crying distracts herself, like a little girl, with her fingers, with a button, with a fly that lands on a friar's nose.

The actors had to be tonsured and grow beards, for artificial ones have been definitively relegated to the theater. And Dreyer's genius lies in the way he directed his actors. In this regard, nothing the cinema has so far given us compares. The humanity in these faces floods the screen and fills the room. We all felt that truth in our throats and in the marrow of our bones—an antidote to snake bites and histrionics! Jannings's acting compared to that of the least of the friars in *The Passion of Joan of Arc* is as bland as lard, and as theatrical—almost—as that of Ludmilla Pitoëff.

And the humanity of the Maid of Orleans spills forth from this work of Dreyer's more than from any other performance we have seen. We all wanted to give her a little thrashing just to be able to hand her a sweet right after. Not letting her have dessert to punish her childish integrity, her transparent stubbornness—that we could see; but why burn her? Spotted with tears, licked by flames, hair cropped short, dirty as a street urchin, still she stops crying for one moment to watch pigeons alight on the church cupola. Then she dies.

We have kept one of her tears, which rolled down to us, in a celluloid box. An odorless, tasteless, colorless tear, a drop from the purest spring.

*From the Spanish. Published in* Gaceta literaria, *no. 43, October 1, 1928.*

# The Comic in Cinema

*The great Cineclub guide, Luis Buñuel, writes on the subject of the up-coming show.*

In my opinion, this is the best and most interesting Cineclub program. It seems that many would have thought of it before, but nonetheless it has never been presented. This should be the cinema program most representative of cinema itself, and purer than all the avant-garde efforts to date. For the minority and the majority, for those uncorrupted by transcendence and art. The finest poems that cinema has produced. Just seeing Harry Langdon or the cross-eyed Ben Turpin go by on the screen is the very pinnacle of happiness, of purification. Of course, to these two-reel films, chosen very selectively, one could add a two-reeler by Charlie and another, again two reels, by Buster. But mixed in at random, without according them any priority over the others. The Charlie of a decade ago could give us great poetic joy. Today he can no longer compete with Harry Langdon. The intellectuals of the world have ruined him, so that now he aims to make us cry with the most vivid commonplaces of feeling. Suarès was the only one, a few years ago now, who dared to speak of "the ignoble heart of Chaplin." It's obvious that this program would be an almost international hit. (I'm thinking here of *Cahiers d'art* and *Du cinéma*, which is the best French cinema magazine.)

Nothing European; all American. No orchestra; gramophone and player piano. No long films; one or two reels.

I think that the show will be something definitive, and it's absurd that none like it has ever been presented at any film society or in any ordinary movie theater in the world. People are so stupid, and have so many prejudices, that they think *Faust, Potemkin,* and the like are superior to these buffooneries, which are not that at all, and which I would call the new poetry. The equivalent of surrealism in cinema can be found only in those films, far more surrealist than those of Man Ray. Ask the young film society members, the Buhigas, and so on, and you will see how excitedly they look forward to this screening.

*At this show, Rafael Alberti will recite poems to the Comics in Cinema.*

*From the Spanish. Published in* Gaceta literaria, *no. 56, April 15, 1929.*

# The Cinematic Shot

*La photographie n'est pour le cinéma*
*qu'un moyen d'expression, sa plume,*
*son encre, sont sa pensée.* *

In the evolutionary process of the visual arts, and even of music, there comes a moment of great importance. These arts have subsisted to that point by feeding on an exhausted tradition, without ever having explored the more potentially fruitful areas specific to their forms of expression. They are submerged in a secular lethargy, and time itself seems to have stopped at the threshold of their evolution. But then an instant arrives when the genius of a new era grants them a new and unimagined vigor. Horizons multiply in succession like waves on the sand, and the concept of art is forever fixed: a chrysalis reaching its moment of definitive perfection.

What the names Cimabue, Giotto, Bach, or Fidias are to other arts, D. W. Griffith is to cinema. Some years ago, this strange grouping of names might have seemed sacrilegious. Today no one would be surprised to find Griffith among the others. He was not only an innovator but the authentic creator of a truly cinematic art. His silhouette neatly frames the history of cinema, which consists of two periods separated by his genius. The first period is as far from art as a color print is from a painted canvas. At most it was a period of trial and error, a period in

---

*[“Photography is merely a means of expression for cinema, while thought is its pen and ink.”—Trans.]

search of its tools, of its brush or its marble, but completely unaware of what it would become. The cinematic era begins in 1913, when Griffith, thanks to his use of the close-up, elevated cinema to a fine art. Today's viewer would be bored with one of the paleolithic films by Griffith. Although they were already cinematic, the other elements that made up these early movies—lighting, actors, set design, etc.—seem mawkish and flawed. For all these elements form a sort of rhetoric of cinema that, moreover, has by now become indispensable; yet the essence and substance of cinematic cinema is, after the lens, the close-up—the brain that thinks and the words that construct and express what has happened.

We call "close-up"—for lack of a better term—anything that results from the projection of a series of images that comment on or explain an aspect of the total view, whether it be a landscape or a person. The filmmaker conceives by means of images distributed in shots. His idea, once realized, is made up of disparate elements that have to be fitted, mixed, and woven together. In other words, the filmmaker is obliged to compose, to inject rhythm, and only then does cinema become art. For if cinema is movement above all, it must be rhythm in order to become cinematic.

If we want merely to record a man running, we will have attained the goal of the motion picture. But what if when we film the race, everything around it disappears and we see only fast-moving feet, then the dizzying landscape and the anguished face of the runner? Through successive shots the lens presents, in abstracted form, the main elements of the race and the feelings created by it; thus we achieve the objective of a cinematic film. It does not simply describe a movement or a sensation—for we identify with the man running—but furthermore, in the harmony of light and shadow, its series of images with their unequal duration and varying spatial relations produces the same pure delight we find in the lines of a symphony or in the abstract forms and volumes of a modern still life. This is how we define the modern tendencies of cinema, which might be called photo cinema, psychological cinema, pure cinema. One variety of this last type is the absolute cinema of Eggeling, such as *Diagonal Symphony*, or of Ruttmann, in which the artist's sole objects are light and shadow in varying intensities, interpolations and juxtapositions of volume, mobile geometries.* There everything is dehumanized. The separation from nature could not be carried any further.

It seems strange to point out that these attempts—not too successfully realized—date from 1919. All the personality that Griffith brought to the cinema, his rapid ascent in the hierarchy of the arts, was, we repeat, due to his use of the close-up. Years before, around 1903, it had first been conceived by Edwin Porter in *The Great Train Robbery*—an unconscious move, not inspired by creative intuition but simply arrived at by chance. We've all seen photographs from that era that portray their model from head to toe, with her bustle or his frock coat and sideburns. One day it occurred to a photographer to bring the camera closer, and from that point on, bust portraits have been in vogue. Edwin Porter played such a role in the history of the close-up shot.

It may seem impertinent to recall that from that first tentative flicker, cinema already possessed most of the technical resources it has today: the iris diaphragm, multiple exposures, *caches*, *volets*, etc.† Its progress, following Griffith's contribution, still relies on the original elements. Very little—if anything—has been created. We can expect these elements to be perfected, but the evolution of the technology is near its end, just as an age of low realism and bad taste is in the making. We are talking about the advent of color and synchronized sound. In these lines we embrace the fellowship of chiaroscuro recently founded in Paris by *Cahiers d'art* critic Bernard Brunius. An infinity of like-minded spir-

---

*[Viking Eggeling (1880–1925) was an avant-garde filmmaker who, with Hans Richter, experimented with abstract forms in film. Walter Ruttmann (1887–1941), a disciple of Eggeling's, was better known as a documentary filmmaker.—Trans.]

†[*Caches*, *volets*: masks, shutters (in French in the Spanish text).—Trans.]

its have placed themselves under the auspices of the muse of silence, wrapped in the pure tunic of chiaroscuro. May its reign endure among people with good taste!

We have seen that the cinema finds its language in the close-up. The lens can express, and multiply proportionally, its wealth of "ideas." Now the true filmic artists can emerge, equipped with an "intelligent" instrument. With them begins the second great shift in cinematic art: one toward intelligence and sensitivity. Thus cinema will forever leave behind the barbaric fair booth to assume its rightful place in its present-day chapels. Barely out of its subterranean phase, its catacombs, this new faith that speaks to everyone in the same language has already spread to every corner of the world. As silent as a paradise, as animistic and vital as a religion, the miraculous gaze of the lens humanizes beings and objects. "A l'écran il n'y a pas de nature morte. Les objets ont des attitudes," said Jean Epstein, the first to speak of this psychoanalytic quality of the lens.*

A close-up of Greta Garbo is no more interesting than that of any object whatsoever, as long as it signifies or defines something in the drama. Forged in the minds of men and held together through their own bodies, the drama too ends up subordinated to things. At a certain point, one of these things can take over all the interest and dramatic significance of the movie. Then the lens aims directly at it, leaving everything else, even the human element, as if it were indeterminate and superfluous. Every shot in a film is the knot—necessary and sufficient—through which the trembling threads of emotion pass. Eliminating the contingent and secondary, it presents in an isolated and intact state all that is necessary and essential. This is one of the great virtues of cinema, one of the true advantages it has over theater.

Let us recall a scene from *The Merry Widow* in which three men gathered in a theater box all desire the same woman, who is dancing across the

*[See page 105n.—Trans.]

stage with graceful spins. Suddenly she stops. According to how she is perceived by each one of the men, the woman is deconstructed into three images: feet, belly, and eyes. Three psychologies are instantly revealed by the lens: a refined sadist, a sexual primitive, and a pure lover. Three psychologies and three motives. The rest of the film is a commentary on those three attitudes. There are as many examples as there are shots. Remember the role played in *Lady Windermere's Fan* by the introductory image or close-up, used frequently, in which two hands trembling with love finally touch.

Griffith gave us the greatest poem of the cinematic shot in 1919 with *Broken Blossoms.** Thereafter, its creator entered into a pronounced decline. As often happens, everyone wanted to imitate him, and for the next four or five years his techniques were excessively abused. Finally, the above-mentioned film by Ernst Lubitsch, *Lady Windemere's Fan*, achieved a balanced use of the technique. Abuse of the close-up, instead of reshaping emotions, diminishes and dilutes them.

It must be kept in mind, moreover, that in a certain sense the concept of the close-up encompasses a wider meaning, that of a shot that must be "edited and given rhythm." Our own filmmakers have not understood this second and analogous meaning, which is the most important, the only one that matters. Not one of our filmmakers takes communion at the altar of Apollo. At most, they snack with Mercury.

Much has been said in recent years about the influence of movies—of the close-up—on art and literature. It might be a product of cinema or the acceleration of the present age, or both things at once. But its existence is irrefutable. For some it happens intuitively. Others establish a method to reach it. Instinctively we would look for the true influence, denuded of literature, in the first group. And indeed there is one among them who deserves special distinction for having created the

---

*[The first film Griffith made after forming United Artists with Douglas Fairbanks, Mary Pickford, and Charlie Chaplin.—Trans.]

close-up in literature. I don't know the date of Ramón's first *greguerías*,\*
but if they preceded 1913 and Griffith knew of them, the influence
of literature over cinema would be undeniable. Sadly or fortunately,
Mr. Griffith probably does not possess a well-stocked library, so for him
Ramón is but one of the many Ramóns who walk the earth.

*From the Spanish. Published in* Gaceta literaria, *no. 7, April 1, 1927.*

.

\*[Ramón Gómez de la Serna (1888–1963) was a prolific Spanish writer
known as the creator, in 1912, of the *greguería*, a brief, acutely observed, some-
times paradoxical prose image of a personal and surprising aspect of reality.—
Trans.]

# *Découpage,* or
# Cinematic Segmentation

Must we first excuse the use of the word *découpage* in place of its Spanish equivalent, *recortar*? Besides being less specific than the French term, our word is less apt for the action it tries to describe. Furthermore, *découpage* is a time-honored word, acquiring an appropriate meaning when used to designate the fundamental preliminary operation in cinema consisting of the simultaneous separation and ordering of the visual fragments contained amorphously in a cinematic *scénario*. It is true that French technical terminology, when applied to cinema, suffers from serious defects and verbal affectation, though it cannot be denied that for years a cultured minority has been interested in cinema and concerned about creating its own vocabulary, to be used to describe its specific techniques. This new vocabulary is starting to replace the old language, which came almost entirely from theater. We need say nothing of America, where the technical terminology is as adequate and useful as its cinematic techniques. But Spain? Our vocabulary was improvised by the most intellectually and industrially bankrupt masses. Therefore, if Spain follows the way of France, or better still America, we can use a vernacular voice; otherwise, if we cease to improvise, as here, with our own resources, we'll have to borrow foreign words rather than accept the linguistically pure terms of our militant cinema: *guión* [script], *rodar* [to shoot], *copión* [combined print], or even worse, *actor*—in cinema there are no actors—and *decoración*—nor is there any decor.

The intuition of film, its cinematic embryo, comes to life in that process called *découpage*. Segmentation. Creation. Excising one thing to turn it into another. What before was not, now is. The simplest and the most complicated way to reproduce, to create. From the amoeba to a symphony. An authentic moment of creation in film is its segmentation. A landscape, to be recreated in film, has to be broken into fifty, a hundred, or more pieces, all of them aligned wormlike, ordering themselves into a colony, composing the film as an entity, the great tapeworm of silence, made up of material segments (*montage*) and ideal segments (*découpage*). The segmentation of segmentation.

A film = A series of shots
A shot = A series of images

An isolated image hardly represents anything. A simple monad, without organization, where evolution stops and starts simultaneously. A direct transcription of the world: the larva of a film. The image is the active element, a cell of invisible action vis-à-vis the shot, the creative element, the one that can direct the colony. Plenty has been said about the role of the shot in the architecture of a film, about its "absolute-spatial" and "relative-temporal" value—its representation and economy of time, through its subordination to other shots. There are even those who weigh all a cinematographer's merits in terms of the so-called rhythm of a film. Although this might be apt in considering a musical, it is less so for cinema in general—for a drama, for example. This use of synecdoche turns an adjectival quality—which only in exceptional cases becomes fundamental—into the essence, the thing itself. Thus *rhythm* and *découpage* are seen as one and the same, which undermines the actual content. The gimmick was not hard to find, since people have continually sought to give cinema the structure and the norms of, or at least some resemblance to, the classical arts, especially music and poetry. This question is just as elastic as that of influence in art. To establish an approximate notion of cinematic art, we must consider two examples of different natures, but simultaneous and inseparable in their representation. Cinematic art = lens + *découpage* + photography + shot. The lens—"that eye without tradition, without morals, without prejudices, but nonetheless able to interpret by itself"—sees the world. The filmmaker then commands it. Machine and man. The purest expression of our time, our art, the real art of every day.

The process of segmentation saves cinema from being merely the photography of animated images. One might argue that a good film that is well shot, with excellent camera angles and performances, would still seem somewhat uncinematic as a whole if it lacked a good *découpage*. It might make a good album of animated photographs, but that is as far from the notion of film as are the sounds of an orchestra tuning up from the symphony that follows. But the opposite can be true: a film with no performers, based wholly on natural objects and made with ordinary photographic techniques, can turn out to be a good film, as the so-called avant-garde filmmakers in France have shown.

The filmmaker—a title reserved only for the creator of the film— is not filmmaking as much during the filming as during the supreme instant of segmentation. Anyone can learn pretty well the basic techniques of cinematography, but only the elect can compose a good film. Through segmentation, the script or the written assemblage of visual ideas ceases to be literature and becomes cinema. There the ideas of the filmmaker are defined, roughly subdivided, cut up, regrouped, and organized. The ideal shots come to life in the same way that a musical piece already exists within the score, complete and decisive, even if no musician ever plays it. Cinema is intuited through meters of celluloid. Emotion glides sinuously like a tape measure. A vulgar adjective can destroy the emotional content of a verse; similarly, two extra meters of film can destroy the emotional content of an image.

Practically speaking, the process of segmentation precedes all the others. Its work requires nothing more than the work of the pen. The whole film, even its best details, is contained on sheets of paper: the interpretation, the camera angles, the length of each segment; here a *fondu enchaîné* or a superimposed close medium shot or long shot, while the camera remains still, pans, or tracks.* The miraculous fluidity of images that spontaneously and uninterruptedly become classified, ordered, and compartmentalized within shots. (Think, feel with images.) Those eyes infused with the evening look at us for a mere instant, less than a second, then extinguish, bleeding into the shadows, in "two turns of the crank, fade out to the end." That soulful hand, a hurricane of hairs, pregnant with unprecedented intentions, disappears in the field of view. The sudden hit of a pan, like the crash of waves, throws us amid the seven deadly sins of the gaze. The universe, the infinite and the minuscule, matter and soul, can navigate within the restrictive confines of the screen—the ocean and a droplet—that traces its rectangle in the brain of a filmmaker like a dimension of his soul.

Some time ago André Levinson published a study about style in filmmaking in which he attributed to editing all the virtues we have described for segmentation. Doubtless he did so because of the great confusion between technical terms and an incomplete understanding of cinematic procedures. Does it matter if sometimes, almost always because of an inadequate *découpage*, defects and errors that should have been anticipated from the start are fixed after the fact by editing? Some people even start filming before they have plotted a single line of their *découpage*, usually out of ignorance, but in a few cases because of excessive practice, thinking too much about what they are about to undertake and creating beforehand a mental *découpage*. The very act of setting one's camera before an object to be filmed presupposes the existence of a *découpage*.

Sometimes in the moment of realization, circumstances arise that make it necessary to improvise, correct, or omit things that had earlier been considered good. The idea of a *découpage*—written or not—is, like the lens, immanent in the notion of film. Editing, by contrast, is simply putting the hand to the plow—the materiality of joining one piece af-

---

*[*Fondu enchaîné:* a dissolve to another scene (in French in the Spanish text).—Trans.]

ter another, coordinating the different shots with each other, removing unwanted images with a scissors. A delicate operation, but extremely manual. However, the guiding idea, the silent procession of images that are concrete, decisive, measured in time and space—in a word, the film —was first projected inside the brain of the filmmaker.

As we have seen, it is clear that only a person with a solid understanding of cinematographic techniques and procedures can efficiently produce the segmentation of a film. Many amateur practitioners of cinema, by assigning numbers in front of each paragraph in their script, think they can grasp the concept of *découpage*. The sad thing is that professionals—with the exception of six or seven people in France, to say nothing of Spain—hold the same ideas about *découpage* as the amateurs.

*From the Spanish. Published in* Gaceta literaria, *no. 43, October 1, 1928.*

# Cinema as an Instrument of Poetry

The group of young people who head the committee for cultural dissemination asked if I would give a lecture. Although I duly thanked them for their attention, I had to turn them down: apart from the fact that I possess none of the qualities required of a lecturer, I feel a keen sense of modesty about speaking in public. Unavoidably, the speaker attracts the collective attention of his listeners and knows that all eyes are upon him. In my case, I can't help feeling a certain embarrassment for fear that they might think me, shall we say, a bit of an exhibitionist. Although this concept I have of the lecturer may be exaggerated or false, the fact that I feel it to be true led me to insist that my period of exhibition be as short as possible, and I proposed the organization of a round table, at which a few friends from different artistic or intellectual fields might comfortably discuss some of the issues concerning the so-called seventh art. Thus it was agreed that the theme would be "cinema as artistic expression," or more concretely, cinema as an instrument of poetry, with all that this latter word holds of a sense of liberation, subversion of reality, a passage into the marvelous world of the subconscious, and nonconformity to the restrictive society that surrounds us.

Octavio Paz once said, "A chained man need only shut his eyes to be able to make the world explode"; paraphrasing him, I would add: the white eyelid of the screen need only reflect the light that is its own to blow up the universe. But for the moment we can sleep peacefully, for the cinematographic light that comes to us is carefully measured and restrained. In none of the traditional arts is there such a great disproportion between the possibilities offered and what has been accomplished. Cinema acts directly upon the viewer in presenting concrete beings and things, isolating him in silence and darkness from what we might call his normal "psychic habitat." For that reason film can captivate him like no other form of human expression. But it can also dull him like no other. Unfortunately, that seems to be the sole mission of the majority of films today: our movie screens make a show of the moral and intellectual emptiness in which cinema thrives, confining itself to imitating novels and theater, except that its means of psychological expression are less rich. It repeats ad nauseam the same stories that the nineteenth century tired of telling, and that are still repeated in contemporary novels.

A moderately cultured individual would reject with scorn a book with one of the plots recounted in the biggest films. Yet, seated comfortably in a dark movie theater, dazzled by the light and movement that exert an almost hypnotic power over him, fascinated by the faces of people and instantaneous scene changes, this same nearly cultured individual placidly accepts the most disparaged clichés.

Thanks to this sort of hypnotic inhibition, the filmgoer loses a significant percentage of his intellectual faculties. I will give one concrete example: *Detective Story*.* The structure of the story is perfect, the director is magnificent, the actors are extraordinary, the production is brilliant, and so on and so forth. But all this talent, all this know-how, all the complex activities that go into the making of a film have been placed at the service of a stupid and remarkably base story. It makes me think of that extraordinary machine in *Opus II*†—a gigantic apparatus made of the finest steel, with a thousand complex gears, tubes, manometers, and levers, as precise as a watch and as imposing as a transatlantic liner— whose sole function was to postmark the mail.

The element of mystery, essential to all works of art, is generally lacking in films. Authors, directors, and producers take great pains not to

---

*[A 1951 film by William Wyler, starring Kirk Douglas.—Trans.]
†[A silent film from the early twenties by Walter Ruttmann.—Trans.]

trouble our peace of mind by closing the marvelous window of the screen to the liberating world of poetry. They would rather have that screen reflect subjects that could be sequels to our everyday life, repeat for the thousandth time the same drama, or make us forget the daily drudgery of work. And all of this sanctioned, naturally, by conventional morality, government censorship, and religion, ruled by good taste and seasoned with bland humor and all the other prosaic imperatives of reality.

Anyone who hopes to see good films will rarely be satisfied by the big-budget productions or by those that come with the approval of the critics and popular acclaim. The personal story, the private individual drama, cannot, in my opinion, interest anyone who is truly alive to his time; if the viewer participates in the joys, the sorrows, the anguish of a character on the screen, it can only be because he sees reflected in them the joys, sorrows, and anguish of society as a whole and, therefore, his own. Unemployment, the uncertainty of daily life, the fear of war, social injustice, and so on are the things that affect all people today, and thus they affect the viewer. But that Mr. So-and-So is unhappy at home and looks around for a girlfriend to distract himself, then finally abandons her to return to his self-sacrificing wife, is undoubtedly moral and edifying, but it leaves us completely indifferent.

On occasion the true essence of cinema springs in an unexpected way from an otherwise trivial film, a slapstick comedy or a banal romance. Man Ray once said something very significant: "The worst films I have ever seen, the kind that put me sound asleep, always have five marvelous minutes in them, and the best films, those most showered with praise, have only five minutes that are worthwhile; in other words, in good films as well as in bad ones, above and beyond and in spite of the director's best intentions, cinematic poetry struggles to come to the surface and reveal itself."

In the hands of a free spirit, the cinema is a magnificent and dangerous weapon. It is the best instrument through which to express the world of dreams, of emotions, of instinct. The mechanism that produces cinematic images is, among all forms of human expression, that which most closely resembles the mechanism of the human mind in the way it works, or better yet, that which best imitates the workings of the mind during sleep. A film is like an involuntary imitation of a dream. Brunius has observed that the night that gradually falls in the movie theater is equivalent to the act of closing the eyes.* It is then that, on the screen and in the depths of the individual, the incursion into the night of the sub-conscious begins. As in dreams, images appear and disappear through dissolves and shadows; time and space become flexible, shrinking and expanding at will; chronological order and relative lengths of time no longer correspond to reality; actions come full circle, whether they take a few minutes or several centuries; movements speed past the delays.

The cinema seems to have been invented to express the life of the subconscious, the roots of which reach so deeply into poetry, yet it is al-most never used toward that end. Among modern film trends, the best known has been called "neorealism." Neorealist films present the viewer with a slice of life, taking characters from the street and even showing actual buildings and interiors. With a few exceptions, among which I would cite in particular *The Bicycle Thief*, neorealism has done nothing to bring out that which is distinctively cinematic, namely, the mysteri-ous and the fantastic. What is the point of all the visual trappings if the situations, the motives that drive the characters, their reactions, and even the plots themselves are drawn from the most sentimental and con-formist literature? The only interesting contribution—brought to us not by neorealism but by Zavattini†—is the raising of the commonplace act to the level of dramatic action. In *Umberto D*, one of the most inter-esting neorealist films, an entire ten-minute reel shows a maid in a se-ries of actions that only a short while ago would have been considered unworthy of the screen. We see the maid go into the kitchen, light the

---

*[Jacques B. Brunius (1906–1967) was a French actor, director, and writer. —Trans.]

†[Cesare Zavattini (1902–1989) was the screenwriter for *The Bicycle Thief* and *Umberto D*, both directed by Vittorio De Sica.—Trans.]

stove, place a saucepan over the fire, throw water several times on a column of ants marching single-file toward the food, take the temperature of an elderly man who feels feverish, and so on. Despite the apparent triviality of these situations, we follow her movements with interest, even with a sense of suspense.

Neorealism has introduced elements into cinematic expression that have enriched its vocabulary, but nothing more. Neorealist reality is incomplete, conventional, and above all rational; poetry, mystery, everything that completes and enlarges tangible reality is entirely missing from its works. Neorealism confuses ironic fantasy with the fantastic and black humor.

"The most admirable thing about the fantastic," André Breton has said, "is that the fantastic doesn't exist; everything is real." Speaking with Zavattini some time ago, I expressed to him my dissatisfaction with neorealism. We were having lunch together, and the first illustration that came to mind was the wineglass I was drinking from. For a neorealist, I said, a glass is a glass and nothing more. We see it being taken from the sideboard, filled with a drink, carried to the kitchen, where the maid will wash it and perhaps break it, which may or may not cause her to be fired, and so on. But this same glass, observed by different human beings, can be a thousand different things, because each person pours a dose of subjective feeling into what he sees, and no one sees it as it really is but as his desires and his state of mind make him see it. I advocate the kind of cinema that will make me see those kinds of glasses, for that cinema will give me a whole view of reality, expand my knowledge of things and people, and open the marvelous world of the unknown, of all that I can't find in the daily press or come across on the street.

Nevertheless, do not think by what I have just said that I favor a cinema exclusively devoted to the expression of the fantastic and the mysterious, an escapist cinema that spurns everyday reality and aspires only to plunge us into the unconscious world of dreams. I have indicated, albeit briefly, the great importance I attach to the film that addresses the fundamental problems of modern man, not considered in isolation, as an individual case, but in relation to others. Let me borrow a few words from Emers. He defined the function of the novelist (and here read film-maker) in this way: "The novelist has acquitted himself honorably of his task when, by means of a faithful rendering of authentic social relations, he has destroyed the conventional view of the nature of those relations, shattering the optimism of the bourgeois world, and has forced the reader to question the permanency of the status quo, even if he does not directly point us to a solution, even if he does not ostensibly take sides."

*From the Spanish. Text of an address delivered at the University of Mexico, Mexico City, December 1958; published in* Universidad de México, *December 1958.*

# Goya and the Duchess of Alba

The year 1788.

The flaming spirit of revolution has reared its head in France, but the people of Spain, docile and pleasure-loving, are more servile than ever toward the crown. Bullfights and fiestas and glorious Spanish sunshine are more to their liking than politics, making them indifferent to their uneasy ministers, who brush aside all inclinations toward a liberal policy.

Soon there will be a new king, Charles IV, a huge, blustering dolt who knows virtually nothing about affairs of state, and whose chief concerns are hunting rabbits and gorging himself with wine and rich food.

Charles is called to the bedside of his father, who is enduring his last illness. The feeble old man tells him about the responsibility of governing a people. Then, somewhat contemptuously, he adds: "Let me warn you about your wife, Maria Louise, who will bring indignity on your name. She's little better than a common harlot, and right under your nose, too."

Charles's stupid countenance darkens in bewilderment. "Why, that's impossible," he blurts out. "It's hard for women of royal rank to commit adultery. There are so few people of equal rank that they have little opportunity . . ."

"What an ass you are, Carlos," sighs the old man in disgust.

Disquieted by his father's words, Charles hastens to Maria Louise, of whose disposition he is in mortal terror. She is far from beautiful, yet the piercing gaze in her lean, pinched features inspires fear and respect. Now she is exasperated before the quailing Charles.

"What!" she exclaims, "Will you accept accusations from a dying old man in his delirium? How dare you suspect my fidelity!"

Charles is both convinced and alarmed. "I'll grant you any favor," he says, "if you'll only calm yourself."

"Very well," she says haughtily, "come here by the window."

Maria Louise points to the courtyard where a very handsome young lieutenant of the guards is parading. He is tall, virile, only eighteen.

"A very talented young man who loves his king and queen," she says softly. "His name is Godoy. I want him as my secretary."

The gullible Charles promises. "As soon as I am made king," he says. More confused than ever, he quits the chamber, leaving the princess standing by the window, her eyes feasting on her next prize.

Now the Duchess of Alba enters the chamber. She is of startling beauty, vivacious, bold, with a wealth of raven tresses framing a delicately carved oval face. "It's tonight," she laughs. "Remember . . . our escapade?"

Maria Louise enjoins her to speak more quietly. Like conspirators they discuss their anticipated adventure. Disguised as ordinary shopwomen, they will saunter into the streets and mingle with the gay throngs that are celebrating a holiday on the outskirts of Madrid. Maybe they can pick up a couple of men . . .

Several hours later, the two women are lost in the crowd of merrymakers. There is gaiety everywhere, with shouting and singing in the festively decorated grove, with men playing flutes, walking on stilts, flirting with all the women within reach. The irrepressible duchess begins to sing, and two *majos*, young toughs from Madrid, begin to flirt with her. Maria Louise is annoyed because she is receiving so little attention. She pretends to be indifferent, even after one of the *majos* grasps her arm. Then the two couples saunter off, headed for a dance hall.

They reach a dark street. The wailing voice of a monk reaches them and they stop to listen. It is someone from the monastic order of Brothers of Mortal Sin, preaching salvation. More quietly now, the party proceeds on its way.

Suddenly they are stopped by a patrol of the *ronda* watchmen. The *majos*, blustering more than ever, are furious, refuse to be questioned. They insult the watchmen, draw their swords, and the terrified ladies flee in opposite directions, with the clash of the swords ringing in their ears.

After a short chase, Maria Louise is caught, and the furious watchman, mistaking her for a woman of the streets, heaps violent abuse upon her. "Who are you?" he demands. Maria Louise tries to conceal her face behind her mantilla, but the watchman rudely tears it away and holds his lantern to her face. Then he steps back in amazement. "The princess!" he mutters, falling at her feet. "Forgive me." Hard, glittering eyes are turned on the unhappy man. "You shall pay," she tells him as she turns away.

Meanwhile, in another direction, the duchess is hotly pursued by another watchman of the *ronda*. He is about to seize her when a sword comes hurtling between his legs, tripping him. The terrified duchess finds herself being led through the darkness by a kindly, burly figure who is holding her arm. They walk quickly with hardly a word between them, until the man opens the door of a house and leads her in.

"This is my home," he says. "You will be safe here."

The duchess is still catching her breath. "Oh, no," she pants. "I won't remain here."

"You must," the man says gently, "at least for a little while. They may still be in the neighborhood." Then he asks, "Were you alone?" "Yes," says the duchess quickly, anxious not to involve Maria Louise. "But I must go now, really."

The man smiles, caresses her hair as the duchess coquettishly pretends to draw away. "You needn't remain very long," he promises, stealing one arm over her shoulder.

The impetuous Goya tries all the tricks of gallantry to win over this charming creature who laughingly persists in behaving like a wary schoolgirl. Though his efforts are seeming in vain, Goya is very pleased. Alba laughs, draws away. For half an hour they fence, with the painter pleading, "Come, at least you ought to be interested in seeing my paintings . . . in the next room."

With his arm still around her he leads her into the atelier where the walls are covered with paintings that are famous all through Spain. The duchess regards them in amazement. "You are Goya!" she exclaims. He nods. The duchess hastily covers her face in alarm, utters a startled cry, and rushes out into the street. Goya tries to pursue her, but the night has swallowed his beautiful, mysterious visitor . . .

The following day finds the vindictive Maria Louise true to type. She hasn't forgotten the misadventure of the previous night, and she hasn't forgotten the watchman who had insulted her. Losing little time, she trumps up a false charge against the unhappy man and has him thrown in prison. "He robbed a poor woman of her purse," she tells the chief justice.

To Charles she tells a different story, a true version except that she substitutes the name of the duchess for her own. "You know how wild the duchess is," she says sweetly. "She shouldn't indulge in such foolish escapades, but of course, no one else must know." Charles, completely taken in, urges her not to become too friendly with such an irresponsible woman.

Meanwhile the romantic Goya, in whose nostrils still lingers the perfume of the woman who had so strangely moved him, searches all Madrid for her. He becomes restless, forgetting everything but the beauty of that woman. As he searches for her, he hears the tolling of church bells proclaiming to the people that the old king is dead.

With traditional ceremony, a new king and queen are crowned. There is grand pomp, wild celebration in the streets of Madrid. Bells ring, games are held, people cavort and shout with glee. In the royal palace there is much ado, with everyone pleased, especially Maria Louise, who has just commanded that Godoy be sent to her as secretary.

Entering her royal presence, the youth is bewildered, awestruck. Dropping to his knees, he is embarrassed as a schoolboy and murmurs to the queen that he has had no training for the job he is to fulfill. "You'll do," says the queen very quietly; "you will learn," she says as the youth continues to protest his inexperience. Unable to restrain herself, the queen lets her fingers steal over his hair while a sigh issues from her lips. Now a subtle change comes over the youth, who is far from stupid. The humble look in his eyes gives way to one of cunning. Raising his head, he is electrified by the enamored look on the face of the queen, and with sudden boldness he springs to his feet and crushes her in his arms . . .

There is ceremony in court. Among those present is Goya, the great court painter who rose from a peasant's rank. He is a large man, warm, passionate, yet retaining the peasant's virtues of simplicity and sincerity. He has just come in, with the Infante Don Luis at his side. Many beautiful women cast their smiles at Goya, as if trying to win his favor.

"You rarely attend these functions," chides Don Luis, "but you should. You must meet the great ladies. First I'll introduce you to the charming Duchess of Alba."

Painter and lady recognize each other instantly, but both are discreet. The duchess regards him haughtily. "You must come to my castle and paint me one day," she says quite formally. Goya, with equal formality, thanks her for the honor and walks off, though his heart is bursting with emotion . . .

Nearly all the great ladies want to be painted by the famous Goya. Legends have sprung up about him, about his appeal to women, about his facility with the brush, how he is able to do a complete portrait in one hour. Even the royal family dotes on him. And in the anteroom of his atelier there are always six or seven ladies waiting patiently for their turn. Often he is obliged to send most of them away.

We see him in his studio, besieged by a marquis and his wife, who is a lady of outstanding beauty. "Please, Goya," begs the marquis, "you must paint my wife today. She has already made several appointments with you."

"I regret exceedingly that I cannot paint her today," the artist says. "I haven't the time, your excellency."

But the marquis is determined. Seizing the key, he rushes outside and locks them in. "Now you are my prisoner!" he shouts through the door. "I'll be waiting here for two hours, and I won't let you out until the job is finished."

When the two hours are up, the marquis opens the door. "Have you finished your job?" he asks. "I have, your excellency," Goya replies, glancing at the lovely marquesa whose face is slightly flushed, while a curious smile hovers about her lips. The marquis looks at the finished portrait. "You have done your job well," he says. "I have, your excellency," replies Goya, very quietly.

Several days go by. Goya hasn't forgotten his promise to paint the Duchess of Alba. Strangely elated, he has his servants carry his equipment to her castle.

Arriving in the grand domicile, he finds her more elusive than ever. Her smile, as he sets up his easel, is ambiguous, both an invitation and a mockery. There they are, the peasant and the lady, with a yawning chasm of tradition and blood between them.

Goya is startled when she cries to him, "No, not that!" She is laughing softly, showing her small white teeth. "I didn't want you to paint my portrait now," she says to him. "I merely invited you up here to paint makeup on my face."

Goya, whose fury when aroused is notorious, clenches his fists and bows respectfully. The duchess, still laughing, fixes him with her eyes, as if daring him to display a temper. But the artist is in control of himself now. Bowing again, he approaches her to perform the humble duty she has asked him.

At length the duchess looks into her mirror, smiles in satisfaction. "Marvelous," she says. "What is your price?" Goya takes her roughly in his arms, kisses her mouth and cheeks with such contemptuous dispatch that the rouge is smeared all over her face. Standing erect with the quiet dignity of which he is capable, Goya laughs in his turn. "That is my price," he says. "So sorry I had to spoil my work." Then he stalks out, leaving the duchess staring ruefully after him, her ego sharply deflated.

The turbulent spirit of war is in the air, and soldiers are being recruited to fight against the French revolutionaries. Louis XVI, a cousin of King Charles, has been beheaded in France, and a wave of fear has swept over the thrones in Europe. The Spanish people, lovers of tradition, are still loyal to the crown, but at any time their sympathies might change.

Godoy, elevated by degrees, is now prime minister of Spain. He is preoccupied and worried. He goes to his mistress, the queen, and tells her he wants to discuss affairs of state. "That can wait," she says. "Come with me, I want to show you something."

Taking his hand, which she fondles, she leads him to her wardrobe chamber.

"Look," she says, "a work of genius. A most special creation from Paris. A dress that will be the envy of everyone, especially that conceited Alba. I am wearing it at her party."

Godoy, unceremoniously, flops on a chair and shrugs his shoulder.

The Duchess of Alba's receptions are a byword in Madrid. Now the great ballroom is lavishly festooned and brilliantly illuminated while a small army of servants deftly move about to care for the guests. On a platform off to one side, members of the orchestra are pompously taking their places waiting for their cue to begin. Alba looks gayer and lovelier than ever, and when she beholds Maria Louise arriving in her new gown she exclaims in delight, "How stunning! How perfectly ravishing it is!"

Others present, not to be outdone, echo her praises, while the queen, with a glint of triumph in her eyes, appears anxious to treat everyone with a glimpse of her gown.

Then Alba signals for the ladies-in-waiting, who come marching in with their trays of refreshments. As they enter, a murmur of amazement sweeps through the ballroom; then all are deathly silent. All the servant girls are wearing exact replicas of the queen's gown!

Maria Louise looks at Alba, her piercing eyes glowing with rage. "It is only a coincidence," she tries to explain. The queen, without uttering a word, storms out of the palace. The other guests don't dare remain.

Mumbling their excuses, they begin to depart. Alba is left standing alone in the center of the room. Her eye falls on the sumptuous food that has been spread on the tables, at the members of the orchestra sitting as if transfixed, at the servants who look embarrassed. Goya crosses the gilded floor to where she is standing. She regards him for a moment, her eyes filled with wonder. Then she reaches out and takes his hand. "You are always around when I am in trouble, my friend," she says simply.

She leads him to the garden, where scented air is stirred by a gentle breeze. Here, beneath the moonlight, as they sit near a plashing fountain, the artist raises her hands to his lips. "I shall always be around when you need me," he says, "but you tempt the queen too much. Why did you do it?"

"The queen and I," Alba replies, "understand each other—with hatred. She hates me because I am young and attractive, and I hate her for being so mean and vindictive."

Drawn irresistibly to him, Alba rests her head on Goya's broad chest. A look of tenderness comes over his face as he tells her, "I will not let you suffer alone."

Alba's smile is wistful. "You are like a great bear," she whispers, "great and lovable. I am sorry if I was ever rude to you. You should be rude to me—you, a man of genius." She sighs.

"Why do you sigh?" he asks.

"I was very rash," Alba tells him. "The queen will answer the insult I gave her."

Goya's arm tightens around her frail body, as if to protect her. Trembling in his embrace, she looks up at him, her eyes wild with love. She is about to fling her arms about his neck when the air is pierced with a cry: "Fire!"

They spring to their feet. Flames are leaping from one corner of the castle as servants pour on it bucket after bucket of water.

"There is her answer!" cries the duchess, as she and Goya watch the vanquishing of the flames.

Meanwhile, from another castle, the queen leans out from her balcony window, beholding the spectacle of the flames. "That," she says slyly to Godoy, who is standing over her, "is probably the judgment of God." Godoy grins understandingly. "Tomorrow," continues the queen, "she will receive my judgment."

The vindictive queen is true to her word. On the following morning the Duchess of Alba is condemned to exile. She is ordered to depart immediately for her castle in Andalusia. The servants are tearful, but Alba as usual is very brave, comforting those who commiserate with her. At last the coach starts, and as it proceeds down the road, she looks back longingly at her beloved Madrid.

The journey is uncomfortable, the road is very bad, mercilessly joggling the duchess. Hour after hour she is subjected to this discomfort until finally, toward dusk, an axle is broken. Coming out of the coach, the duchess finds that the air is very cold. She shivers as her servants tell her that they might not get help before morning. Two of them go on ahead in search of a blacksmith.

Suddenly, Alba utters a shout of joy. She sees coming toward her a solitary horseman—Goya. Leaping from his mount, he cries out to her, "I couldn't let you make this trip alone, my duchess. I'll go into exile with you!" "But your career," she says, "what about your career?" Goya whispers fervently, "You will be my career. I'll paint so many portraits of you that all the world will ring of your beauty!"

Alba enjoins him to walk with her a short distance, away from the prying ears of the servants. Forgetting the cold and the hours as they pass, the lady and the peasant at last yield utterly to the passion that draws them together. Locked in each other's embrace they swear eternal love, love that will transcend all barriers, even the one of social caste. Her protestations of love are as vehement as his own; she assures him that she loved him from the very first moment of their meeting, even though she had not previously dared to acknowledge it. At last Goya realizes that she is shivering with cold.

"You cannot stay here. You must go on. And I with you," he laughs.

"We shall never be parted again, my Francisco," she tells him, "but we cannot go on yet. The axle . . ."

Goya grunts masterfully. "You rest in the coach where it is warm," he says. "I'll fix the axle and we will go on."

While the duchess, exhausted now, sleeps in the coach, Goya sets about to repair the axle. Taking off his coat, he builds a fire and improvises a forge. Hour after hour he works, ignoring the chill that is creeping through his perspiring skin.

But he labors in vain. Overcome with fatigue and the frigid cold, he approaches the duchess in the coach, discovers she is asleep. Several heavy blankets cover her delicate body, but Goya refuses to touch them. His chilled hands fish under the coach for a thin bit of canvas. This he takes to cover himself as he lies down to sleep near the fire.

A storm comes up. Rain beats down on Goya and extinguishes the fire. Huddled under his canvas he spends a miserable night trying to sleep. Morning. The duchess, rousing herself, calls to Goya, but he does not reply. Hurrying over to him she calls again, receives no response, and discovers to her horror that he is deaf. Exposure has made him quite ill. He is feverish, delirious.

The duchess is frantic. Then she receives another shock. Five horsemen come galloping up and seize the sick man.

"King's orders," says the captain gruffly. "Goya is needed in Madrid as court painter."

"You cannot take him," Alba says fiercely. "I forbid it."

"Sorry," says the captain more politely. "I am powerless. It's the king's orders."

The duchess is beside herself. "King's orders! The queen's, you mean. That lustful old witch! She'll do anything to make me miserable."

But she is powerless. Left alone now, she screams, "Francisco! I love you! Come back to me!"

It is a love-maddened, sullen Goya that the doting court has now to contend with. Though still respectful to the royalty who are keeping him from his love, his manner is almost that of a hurt child. Even Godoy is moved.

He has just finished a portrait of Godoy.

"Wonderful" says the prime minister. "You may have any price you ask."

As he speaks we see Goya watching his lips, for the painter is partially deaf.

"Any price," he repeats slowly. "Would the pardon of the duchess be asking too much?"

Godoy is very sympathetic. He places a hand on Goya's shoulder.

"I wish I could," he says sincerely. "But it's the queen who sent her away, and only the queen can pardon her."

Goya is in despair. Even the prospect of the greatest commission of his career, the painting of the entire royal family, doesn't seem to interest him. He knows the vanity of his royal patrons, how each of them will crowd for a favorable position on the canvas. Even Maria Louise is excited about the work he has commenced.

All the court is discussing its progress. Day after day his subjects go to their places with the eager interest of schoolchildren. Goya becomes animated again, is actually cheerful.

At last the painting is finished, all but the faces.

"When will you paint the faces?" the king and queen want to know.

There is a cunning gleam in Goya's eye, even though his manner is more respectful than ever.

"Oh, tomorrow, probably, your majesties," he says. "But first I would like to speak to you if you will permit it."

They wait for him to speak. His manner has become crafty.

"You know, your majesties," he says very humbly, "that the mind and hand of an artist must be free of all obsessions if he is to do full justice to his art."

They regarded him uncomprehendingly.

"My spirit would have the freedom it needs if my mind were no longer disturbed about one thing," he goes on, "—the pardon of the Duchess of Alba."

The queen glares at him, while the face of Charles is blank as ever.

"And," continues Goya, "without the pardon the portrait might suffer. There is good reason to believe that I might not even be able to go on with it at all."

"That's impudent," exclaims the queen.

"That's art, your majesty," Goya replies. "An artist is often imprisoned by his emotions." He gestures helplessly.

"You speak of imprisonment," snaps the exasperated queen. "I'll show you the inside of a real prison, one that has no art."

"If you imprison me, your majesty," says Goya intrepidly, "posterity will not profit by the picture of your great family."

The queen is furious.

At last Charles asserts himself. "We must have the painting," he says to the queen. "Why, it's nearly finished. Anyway, you've punished Alba enough."

"I won't pardon that woman," snaps the queen.

The vain Charles glances at the painting that is nearly completed. Over his stupid face there suddenly comes a look of resolution. Even the queen is impressed. "You want that painting as much as I do," he says with some force. "Alba will be pardoned."

"She will not!" screams Maria Louise.

Charles puffs himself up, speaks from his great height. "I am still the king. She will be pardoned." The queen knows she's beaten, and shrugs her shoulders.

We see Charles signing the pardon and handing it to Goya. Then he calls him aside. "After you finish this picture," he says greedily, "will you paint one of me alone, a big one in my best uniform? You'll do that, eh?"

Goya is overjoyed. "I'll paint three of them," he assures Charles.

The family portrait is finished. With the writ of pardon secure on his person, Goya starts out for Andalusia. Off to his beloved duchess he goes, the memory of their last passionate meeting still fresh in his memory. He spurs on his horses, an artist-lover hurrying to his greatest glory.

He arrives at the castle in Andalusia. Alba's greeting puzzles him. She is cordial, but hardly more than that. When Goya arrives, she is sitting in her garden with a small party of aristocrats and bullfighters. And she seems very attentive to one of the bullfighters, Costillares, a very famous one.

"You are pardoned," Goya tells her. "You may return to Madrid."

The duchess laughs gaily. Once again she has become the great lady, worldly, frivolous. "Really?" she says to Goya. "How good of Maria Louise. You must come."

In the presence of these people, Goya suddenly feels dismally alone. Somehow he is made to feel a peasant who is graciously welcomed in good society. Is this the Duchess of Alba who embraced him so fervently at their last meeting?

At the bullfight Costillares puts on a grand show. Goya observes that the duchess is completely enthralled, and when she throws a flower to the hero a slight groan escapes from Goya's lips. Now Costillares executes the veronica, which he has invented, and the duchess appears overcome with admiration. Goya can stand no more. Very quietly he rises and leaves.

Costillares in the ring is magnificent. Cheering and wild applause reward his virtuosity with the cape, and after each veronica he looks up to receive a warm smile from the duchess. At last he kills the bull. Looking up again, the triumphant expression on his face is frozen. The duchess is no longer smiling; she is not even looking at him. She has just discovered that Goya has disappeared.

It is a gay group that returns to the palace of Alba for celebration. There is drinking and bright chatter in the sumptuous dining room as the servants bring in the platters of food. But the gaiety of Alba seems strained. She has just learned from her servants that Goya has departed for Madrid.

"You seem preoccupied," says Costillares, placing his hand on her arm in a friendly manner. He is surprised when she impatiently brushes his hand away. Then she is contrite. "Forgive me," she says. "I am terribly annoyed."

Alba stands by the window, her eyes glued to the road that leads to Madrid. In her ears there is dinned the sounds of laughter and merry quips of her guests. Suddenly a look of weariness and disgust pinches her lovely features, and she turns abruptly on her guests. Her voice breaking with irritation, she tells them that she is feeling very ill, that they will have to leave at once. And not many minutes elapse before we find the unhappy Alba standing alone in the center of the room, while in the background her servants stare dismally at the unconsumed repast on the table.

Goya, disillusioned, has become a recluse. Except for solitary walks at night, he has shut himself off from the world, and even his closest friends cannot get to him.

We see two of them knocking in vain at the door of his atelier.

"I know he's inside," says one. "I saw his light from across the street."

"Something terrible has happened to his soul," says the other sadly. "Poor Goya. He just stays here, painting those blasphemous Caprichos, poking fun at the crown and the church. They will put him in prison."

"Worse than that, if the Inquisition gets to him. Already they are scheming to get him in their clutches. Then it will mean torture— death . . ."

"Oh, well, the king will go on protecting him."

"Yes, but for how long? That dreadful Inquisition!"

Goya, inside, is painting one of his Caprichos. Partly deaf, he doesn't hear at first the rapping at his door. But the rapping becomes louder, insistent. At last he turns around, walks to the door, mutters that he doesn't wish to see anybody. As he turns away the rapping continues. With a gesture of extreme annoyance, Goya pulls open the door and beholds the Duchess of Alba!

Boiling with emotion, he refuses to let her in. "Your place is with your aristocratic friends," he says fiercely as he closes the door. "I no longer wish to aspire to your level."

Returning to his easel his sits in gloom, his shoulders hunched in misery.

That night he takes his wonted walk. From the darkness three masked men spring upon him. The powerful artist battles valiantly until one of his assailants, a tall man with a short pointed beard, fells him with a cruel blow to the side of the head. Blindfolded and trussed, Goya is led away.

He is taken to the palace of Alba. It is her hands that undo the blindfold as he stands, still trussed up, tied upright to a pillar.

"You!" Goya exclaims, and he heaps upon her a tirade of fury. Alba is equally furious. "You resort to such methods!" Goya blurts out. "Your stubborn nature requires such methods," she retorts. Then they belabor each other with a storm of imprecations, while Goya, helpless, struggles in his bonds.

Then Alba explains to him that he was wrong to have been jealous. A lady of her station couldn't fly into his arms and betray great emotion. Of course she was grateful, Alba says, and she loved him too. Then why be jealous of the others, who were only friends? Goya, still bitter, is not impressed. "You think I don't love you!" cries the duchess. Goya is silent. A look of exasperation comes over her face. She slaps him several times. Then, beholding him mute and helpless in his bonds, the rage in her collapses. Now, overwhelmed with tenderness, she embraces him passionately, cries, "I love you." Their lips meet in a kiss.

Some time later they sit close together, her hands in his. "Let me prove my love," says Alba passionately. "Here, in Madrid, our different stations make it so difficult. Let us flee Madrid where our love won't be poisoned by the rigid walls of caste."

Goya tells her that her sacrifice would be too great, and he cannot abandon his career as a painter. Now he is convinced of her love. They will remain in Madrid.

As he leaves the castle, Goya recognizes one of the servants by his short pointed beard, the tall man who had brutally knocked him down. With one blow of his fist, Goya sends the man sprawling. Then, lifting him up bodily, he suspends him by his pants to the bough of a tree.

We next see Goya in his studio, finishing a portrait of Alba. She dips a brush into the oil and paints two rings on the hand of her portrait—the symbol of betrothal. On these rings she inscribes the names Alba and Goya.

Godoy's chamber. The duchess comes to him. She is accompanied by her pet, a mischievous little Negro girl of four.

The duchess asks Godoy to secure pardon for one of her servants who has been guilty of a petty misdemeanor. While they speak, the little Negro girl idles about the room, picks up a sheet of paper that has been lying on the desk. This the child twists into a doll's hat.

Back in the carriage, the child proudly shows it to her mistress. The duchess, amused at first, observes writing on the paper hat. As she reads, her eyes widen. This is an incriminating letter, written by Maria Louise to Godoy, mentioning their love child. A sly look comes over Alba's face. Folding the letter carefully, she places it in her bodice.

Godoy, missing the letter, goes to the queen in alarm. They quarrel violently when Maria Louise accuses him of negligence. "Anyway," the queen says furiously, "this time the duchess has gone too far. She will never annoy me again."

Several days later, Goya is working in his studio when the duchess bursts in on him. She is breathless, thoroughly alarmed.

"We must leave Madrid," she says, "and we must not delay."

"But I cannot leave my work," says Goya. "I thought we had agreed . . ."

Alba tells him that her life is in imminent danger. "I have just learned," she says, "that Maria Louise means to have me killed."

Goya's manner changes instantly. "Then we will leave, of course," he says.

They agree to depart on the following day. Alba returns to her palace after her lover agrees to call for her next morning.

That night a terrible storm breaks out. Rain and a howling wind rage outside while Goya lies in his bed, unable to sleep. As if visited by a fore-boding of evil, his face is contorted with fear and doubt. Once he cries out, "Who is there?" and springs from his bed only to discover that he is quite alone. Just as he crawls back into bed a fierce gust of wind knocks down a portrait of Alba. Goya hastens to set the portrait upright. As he stumbles about the room in his agitation, he hears a furious knocking at his door. He opens it.

One of Alba's servants comes in, drenched to the skin, his teeth chat-tering with cold and fright. "Come at once," he says, "the duchess is dying."

Goya rushes to the bedside of his love.

Still stunned by the news, he gazes in bewilderment at the assembly of servants, the weeping little Negro girl, the physicians, and the notary who listens carefully as Alba dictates terms of her will.

Goya violently seizes one of the servants. "Tell me quickly," he de-mands. "What has happened?"

"The physician thinks it is poison," the servant tells him.

The duchess, raising her eyes, sees Goya, calls to him. As he plunges forward her arms rise feebly as if to embrace him. "Francho!" she cries as he falls to her side and presses her hand to his face.

The physician tries to make Goya leave, but the duchess restrains him, says she wishes to be alone with the painter. In a few moments the others clear the room.

Alba's eyes flutter open as she smiles faintly. "Still the same Francho," she says, "always around when I'm in trouble."

Goya groans. "I'll be around with you for ever, from now on," he whis-pers, as his hand moves significantly to his sword. The dying woman places a restraining hand on his arm. "No, no," she gasps. "You must not die." She makes him promise that he will go on living for the sake of his immortal art. Even though he goes on living, she tells him they will still be united in love, for his portraits of her had blended them in a marriage of the spirit for all posterity. Fighting back his tears, Goya slips a ring from his finger, and places it on the finger of Alba, next to the one she is wearing.

We see those two rings on her limp hand . . .

Then that hand becomes the hand of the portrait of the Duchess of Alba . . .

We draw away from the portrait, our attention receding in space and time, we behold a very old Goya, aged eighty, reverently contemplating the same hand.

The aged genius at last draws his eyes away. He is nearly stone deaf, employs the use of a trumpet when his servants address him. He wears two pairs of thick spectacles and his body is quite feeble, but he hasn't lost all of his old fire. He is still brusque and impatient with his servants, but there is an element of mellowness and humor in his old eyes.

One of his servants straightens the blanket over his legs and announces that his physician is coming. Goya exclaims with some heat, "What, that old fool again!"

The physician understands Goya's temperament. He both chides and humors him while performing the routine of looking at his tongue, examining his pulse, etc. The physician says, "You persist in disobeying me, you old rogue. Your servant tells me you demanded mutton yesterday." "I have no prejudice against mutton," says Goya calmly. "But I have," the physician tells him, "for your table. Good broth is what you need." "Broth," scoffs the old man, "I wouldn't wash my paintbrushes in it."

The physician has just tested his patient's reflexes. Then he takes Goya's hand in his own. "Now squeeze," he orders, "as hard as you can." The painter squeezes and there comes over the face of the physician a look of intense pain. He is glad when Goya releases him. "Bah!" he exclaims, "still strong as a mule. I guess you'll live forever."

A subtle change comes over Goya's face. "I may not," he says, "I don't know." His eyes travel back to the portrait of the duchess. As he gazes at the picture his face becomes exalted. "But she will. I know that."

THE END

*Original English text, written as a synopsis for Paramount in 1937.*

# Un Chien andalou

*The publication of this screenplay in* La Révolution surréaliste *is the only one I have authorized. It expresses, without any reservations, my complete adherence to surrealist thought and activity.* Un Chien andalou *would not exist if surrealism did not exist.*

*A box-office success, that's what most people think who have seen the film. But what can I do about those who seek every novelty, even if that novelty outrages their most profoundly held convictions, about a sold-out or insincere press, about this imbecilic crowd that has found* beautiful *or* poetic *that which, at heart, is nothing other than a desperate, impassioned call for murder?*

### Prologue

Once upon a time . . .

A balcony at night. Near the balcony, a man sharpens his razor. The man looks at the sky through the window and sees . . .

A thin cloud moving toward the full moon.

Then the head of a young woman, her eyes wide open. The blade of a razor moves toward one of her eyes.

The thin cloud now passes in front of the moon.

The razor blade runs across the young girl's eye, slicing it.

END OF THE PROLOGUE

Eight years later.

A deserted street. It's raining.

A character, dressed in a dark gray suit, appears on a bicycle.

His head, shoulders, and back are wrapped in white cloth mantelets.

On his chest, held fast with straps, is a rectangular box with black-and-white diagonal stripes. The character pedals mechanically, leaving the handlebars free, his hands resting on his knees.

The character is seen from behind down to the thighs in a close medium shot, superimposed over the length of the street in which he rides with his back to the camera.

The character advances toward the camera until the striped box is seen in close-up.

A nondescript room on the third floor above the same street. In the middle of the room sits a young woman wearing a vibrantly colored dress and attentively reading a book. She suddenly gives a start, listens with curiosity, and gets rid of the book by tossing it onto a nearby couch. The book remains open. On one of the pages we see an engraving of *The Lacemaker* by Vermeer. The young woman is convinced now that something is going on; she stands up, turns around, and quickly approaches the window.

The character seen a moment ago has just come to a stop in the street below. By inertia, without putting up the least resistance, he falls into the gutter with his bicycle, right into a pool of mud.

With a gesture of anger, of spite, the young woman rushes downstairs and out into the street.

Close-up of the expressionless character stretched out on the ground in the exact position he was in at the moment of his fall.

The young woman exits the house and rushes toward the cyclist, kissing him frantically on the lips, the eyes, the nose.

The rain intensifies to the point of obliterating the preceding scene.

Fade in with the box, its diagonal lines superimposed on those of the rain. Hands holding a small key open the box and remove a tie wrapped in tissue paper. It must be noted that the rain, the box, the tissue paper, and the tie all are shown with diagonal lines that vary only in width.

The same room.

Standing next to the bed, the young woman looks at the accessories worn by the character—mantelets, box, and a stiff collar with a dark, plain tie—all arranged as if worn by someone stretched out on the bed. The young woman decides finally to pick up the collar, from which she removes the plain tie and replaces it with the striped one that she has just taken from the box. She puts it back in the same place, then sits down next to the bed in the manner of someone keeping vigil over a corpse. (*Note:* The bed, that is to say, the cover and pillow are lightly rumpled and depressed, as if in fact a human body were lying there.)

The woman has the feeling that someone is behind her, and she turns around to see who it is. Without the slightest surprise, she sees the character, this time without any accessories, who watches something intently in his right hand. His rapt attention turns to distress.

The woman approaches and sees for herself what he has in his hand.

Close-up of the hand, in the center of which ants crawl as they emerge from a black hole. Not a single one falls.

Fade in on the armpit hair of a young woman stretched out on the sunlit sand of a beach. This fades into a sea urchin whose movable spines vibrate gently. This in turn fades into the head of another young woman shot steeply from above, encircled by the iris diaphragm. The iris widens to reveal that this young woman is in the midst of a group of people who are trying to break through a police cordon.

In the center of the circle, she uses a stick to try to pick up a severed hand with painted fingernails that is lying on the ground. One of the policemen approaches and scolds her sharply; he bends down and picks up the hand, which he carefully wraps and places in the box that the cyclist was carrying. He gives the whole thing to the young woman, whom he salutes militarily as she thanks him.

It should be noted that when the policeman gives her the box, she is overcome by an extraordinary emotion that completely isolates her from everything. It's as if she were subdued by distant strains of religious music, perhaps music she heard in her earliest childhood.

The crowd, its curiosity satisfied, begins to disperse in all directions.

This scene has been watched by the characters we left in the room on the third floor. We see them through the windows of the balcony, from which the end of the scene described above may be viewed. When the policeman gives the box back to the young woman, the two characters on the balcony also seem overcome by the same emotion, an emotion that brings them to tears. Their heads sway as if following the rhythm of that barely perceptible music.

The character looks at the young woman, making a gesture to her that seems to say: "You see? Didn't I tell you?"

She looks again into the street, at the young woman who is now alone, as if pinned in place in a state of absolute inhibition. Cars pass by at vertiginous speeds. Suddenly one of them runs her over, mangling her horribly.

Then, with the decisiveness of a man completely within his rights, the character approaches the young woman and, after looking lasciviously into the whites of her eyes, he grabs her breasts through her clothes. Close-up of lascivious hands on her breasts, which emerge from under her dress. We then see a nearly fatal expression of anguish reflected in the character's features. Blood-streaked drool runs from his mouth onto the young woman's uncovered chest.

The breasts disappear and transform into thighs that the character continues to feel up. His expression has changed. His eyes gleam with wickedness and lust. His wide-open mouth closes, becoming minuscule, as if tightened by a sphincter.

The young woman backs off into the room, followed by the character, still with the same expression.

With a sudden forceful gesture she throws off his arms, thus freeing herself from the contact underway.

The character's mouth contracts in anger.

She senses that an unpleasant or violent scene is about to take place.

She backs off, step by step, until she reaches a corner, where she takes refuge behind a small table.

The character gestures like the traitor in a melodrama. He looks everywhere, searching for something. At his feet he sees a length of rope and picks it up with his right hand. He gropes with his left hand and grasps an identical rope.

The young woman, pressed against the wall, watches her aggressor's little game in horror.

He advances toward her, dragging along, with great exertion, whatever is attached to the ropes.

First we see a cork go by, then a melon, two Christian friars, and finally two grand pianos. The pianos are filled with the corpses of donkeys, whose feet, tails, hindquarters, and excrement overflow the insides of the pianos. As one of these pianos passes by the lens, we see the large head of a donkey resting on the keyboard.

The character pulls this load with great difficulty, straining desperately toward the young woman. He overturns chairs, tables, a floor lamp, etc. The hindquarters of the donkeys bump into everything. The light fixture hanging from the ceiling, jostled by the passing of a fleshless bone, swings until the end of the scene.

When the character is about to reach the young woman, she evades him with a leap and runs away. Throwing down the ropes, her assailant sets off after her. The young woman opens a door and disappears into the adjacent room, but not quickly enough to lock herself in. The character's hand, having gotten past the jamb, is trapped there, caught at the wrist.

Inside the room, pushing harder and harder against the door, the young woman watches the hand contract painfully in slow motion, and the ants reappear and scatter on the door. Immediately she turns her head toward the interior of the new room, which is identical to the previous room but appears somehow different because of the lighting; the young woman sees . . .

The same bed, on which the character whose hand is still caught in the door is stretched out, dressed in the mantelets and the box on his chest, without making the slightest gesture, his eyes wide open and with a superstitious expression that seems to say: "Now something truly extraordinary is about to happen!"

*About three o'clock in the morning.*

A new character, seen from behind, has just stopped on the landing near the door to the apartment where these events have taken place. He rings the doorbell. We see neither the bell nor the electric knocker, but through two holes above the door where they would have been, we see two hands rocking a silver martini shaker. Their action is instantaneous, as in ordinary films, when the doorbell is rung.

The character gives a start in bed.

The young woman goes to open the door.

The newcomer goes straight to the bed and imperiously orders the character to get up. He complies so sourly that the other finds himself obliged to grab him by the mantelets and force him to stand up.

After tearing off the mantelets one by one, he throws them out the window. The box follows, along with the straps, which the patient tries in vain to save from the catastrophe. This leads the newcomer to punish the character by sending him to stand against one of the walls of the room.

The newcomer will have executed all these movements with his back to the camera. He turns around for the first time to go look for something on the other side of the room.

At that moment the photography becomes hazy. The newcomer moves in slow motion and we see his features, identical to those of the character; they are one and the same, except that the latter has a younger, more pathetic air, as the former must have had some years ago.

The newcomer goes toward the back of the room, preceded by the camera, which he follows in a close medium shot.

A desk comes into view, and our individual moves toward it. Two books and various school things are on the desk; their positions and moral import will be determined with care.

He picks up the two books and turns to go back to the character. At that moment everything returns to normal; the soft focus and slow motion cease.

Stopping next to him, he tells him to stretch out his arms, places a book in each hand, and orders him to stay that way as punishment.

The punished character now has a sharp expression, full of treachery. He turns toward the newcomer. The books, which he continues to hold, transform into revolvers.

The other looks at him with tenderness, at times increasingly so.

The character of the mantelets, threatening the other with his weapons, forces him to put his hands up and, despite the latter's compliance, fires both revolvers at him. In a close medium shot, the newcomer falls, mortally wounded, his face contorted in pain (the soft focus returns and the fall forward takes place in a slow motion more pronounced than before).

From a distance we see the wounded man fall, but this time he is not in the room but in a park. Seated motionless at his side, seen from behind, is a woman with bare shoulders leaning slightly forward.

As he falls, the wounded man tries to grasp and caress the shoulders. One of his hands, trembling, is turned toward himself; the other brushes lightly over the skin of the bare shoulders. He falls finally to the ground.

View from a distance. Some passersby and a few park keepers rush over to help him. They lift him in their arms and carry him through the woods.

The mad, limping man comes onto the scene.

And we return to the same room. A door—the one in which the hand had been caught—opens slowly. It's the young woman we know. She closes the door behind her and looks very intently at the wall against which the murderer had stood.

He is no longer there. The wall is intact and without a single piece of furniture or decoration.

The young woman makes a gesture of impatience and pique.

We again see the wall, in the center of which is a small black stain. Seen closer, this small stain is a death's-head moth. Close-up of the moth.

The death's-head on the wings of the moth fills the entire screen.

In a close medium shot, the man of the mantelets suddenly appears. He hurriedly raises his hand to his mouth, like someone about to lose his teeth. The young woman looks at him with contempt.

When the character takes away his hand, we see that his mouth has disappeared. The young woman seems to say to him, "Fine. So what?" and touches up her lipstick.

We see the character's head once again. Hair begins to grow where his mouth used to be.

On noticing this, the young woman stifles a cry and looks quickly at one of her armpits, which is completely depilated. Scornfully she sticks her tongue out at him, throws a shawl over her shoulders, and opening the door next to her, walks into the adjacent room, which is a vast beach.

Near the water, a third character waits for her. They greet each other very amiably and walk along the edge of the surf.

A shot of their legs and the waves unfurling at their feet.

The camera follows them on a dolly. The waves gently wash up at their feet first the straps, then the striped box, the mantelets, and finally the bicycle. This view continues for a moment longer without the sea offering anything further.

They continue their walk on the beach, fading little by little as these words appear in the sky:

IN THE SPRING

Everything has changed. Now we see a limitless desert. Stuck in the center of it, buried up to their chests in the sand, we see the main character and the young woman, blind, their clothes in tatters, devoured by the rays of the sun and by a swarm of insects.

*From the French. Published in* La Révolution surréaliste, *no. 12, December 15, 1929.*

# L'Age d'or

## Scenario

Scorpions live in the rocks. Having climbed atop one of these rocks, a bandit sights a group of archbishops, who sing while seated in the mineral landscape. The bandit hurries to announce to his friends the presence, right nearby, of the Majorcans (the archbishops). When he gets to his hut, he finds his companions in a strange state of weakness and depression. They take up their weapons and leave, with the exception of the youngest, who cannot even get up. They set out among the rocks, but one after the other they fall to the ground, unable to go on. Then the leader of the bandits collapses without hope. From where he lies, he hears the sea and sees the Majorcans, who are now reduced to skeletons scattered among the stones.

An enormous marine convoy comes ashore at this steep and desolate spot. The convoy consists of priests, soldiers, nuns, ministers, and sundry civil servants. All head toward the place where the remains of the Majorcans lie. In imitation of the authorities leading the procession, the crowd takes off their hats.

They have come to found imperial Rome. The first stone is being laid when piercing cries draw everyone's attention. In the mud close by, a man and a woman struggle amorously. They separate the two. They strike the man, and the police carry him off.

This man and woman will be the main characters of the film. Thanks to a document that reveals his high status and the important humanitarian and patriotic mission entrusted to him by the government, the man is soon set free. From that moment on, all his efforts are directed toward

Love. In the course of an unrealized love scene, characterized by the violence of its abortive acts, the protagonist is called on the telephone by the important person who had put him in charge of the humanitarian mission in question. This minister denounces him. Because he has abandoned his task, thousands of old people and innocent children have perished. The film's protagonist greets this accusation with insults and, without listening further, returns to his beloved's side just as a completely inexplicable accident succeeds in separating her from him even more definitively. Afterward we see him throw out the window a flaming fir tree, an enormous farm implement, an archbishop, a giraffe, some feathers—all at the exact instant when the survivors from the chateau of Selligny cross the snow-covered drawbridge. The Count of Blangis is clearly Jesus Christ. This final episode is accompanied by a *pasodoble*.*

*From the French. Written in 1930.*

---

*We also see in this film, among other things, a blind man being abused, a dog being crushed, a son nearly killed gratuitously by his father, an old lady being slapped, etc.

# Gags

1. In the dead of night, someone is trying to force open a window outside the castle. He finally manages to break the lock and enters with extreme caution. The hall is pitch-dark. The intruder switches on his flashlight and begins to shine it around the room, but at that very moment someone turns on the lights. Stretched out on the floor, on the armchairs, on the staircase of the hall more than two hundred soldiers lie sleeping. A few of them wake up and complain. "Turn off the light." "Let us sleep." "What a lame joke." Flabbergasted, the intruder smiles sheepishly and climbs back out the window. They don't stop him because no one can imagine that with two hundred watchmen there a thief might enter.

2. The owners of the castle and their guests, some six or seven people in all, climb the staircase of the main hall to go to bed. In the corridor on the second floor, where various doors lead to their rooms, they bid one another good night and retire. A short while later, one of the guests cautiously leaves his room on a mysterious expedition. As he approaches the staircase he hears the nearby voices of people coming up the stairs. They are exactly the same people as before, who again say good night and retire to their rooms.

3. In the middle of the night someone stands in front of a strongbox trying to break it open. Suddenly he sees a flicker of light and hears footsteps. He sees one of the guests coming toward him with a lit candle.

There is no time to hide. But the girl walks past him indifferently. She's sleepwalking. The thief breathes a sigh of relief. The girl disappears through the curtain of a nearby doorway. As soon as she is out of the thief's view, she sets the candlestick down on a chair and turns to observe the thief cautiously from behind the folds of the curtain.

4. In the still of the night, a strange noise is heard in the garden, as if someone were kicking a sound box. A guest peers out from the window of his room. He sees a guy kicking along a violin. Finally, with intense rage, he stomps the instrument flat.

5. A heavy knock at the castle door creates a moment of great tension. They go to open it. In the frame of the door Napoleon appears in his characteristic pose. Taking advantage of their surprise at his appearance, he enters, climbs the stairs, and disappears from the view of the stupefied guests.

6. There is a well-known gag in which a man arrives at the castle and urgently requests an audience with the castle lord. The butler offers him a chair in the vestibule and tells him to sit and wait. A moment later the same butler returns and asks him to please be so kind as to follow him. The visitor, still seated, does not answer. The butler insists but gets no response. He touches the visitor's shoulder, and the visitor falls to the floor in an inert mass. He's dead. This gag is identical except that upon falling to the floor the visitor wakes up and, furious, slaps the butler in the face. He was only sleeping.

7. Someone in the midst of a struggle or in a moment of danger fires a shot from a revolver. The bullet, as if in a dream, exits the gun very slowly and falls at the feet of the one who fired it. This fills the person with terror. He wants to flee but can't. It's as if he were nailed to the ground.

8. We see from a distance, without hearing what they're saying, the leading man and the star playing cards. Her expression betrays her boredom, his a frivolous interest in the game. Now in close-up, their conversation can be heard. It is the most passionate romantic dialogue imaginable. "What terrible anguish, my love, to always have to dissimulate." "Only death will unite us forever." "I adore you." "And not to be able to take you in my arms, to kiss your eyes, your lips a thousand times . . ." As she is about to pick up the cards to deal, he places his hand on hers. "I die of pleasure at the mere touch of your hand." We see them again from a distance and get the impression that he is telling her, quite harshly, that it's his turn to deal. There are a number of witnesses to this scene; hence, their need to dissimulate.

9. On the mantel or atop a piece of furniture is a magnificent portrait of a bride with a white veil and orange blossoms. Someone asks who she is. She's the daughter of the castle lord. She died fifteen years ago, under tragic circumstances, on the very day of her wedding. Later, in the middle of the night, while the rain whips the trees in the garden, we see the image of the bride—but in flesh and blood, her wedding dress drenched with rain, looking sadly toward the castle. Hands cover her mouth and pull her out of sight.

10. Someone, the detective for example, is inspecting the castle. Suddenly his attention is drawn to voices and noises coming from one of the rooms. He approaches and finds that the door is locked. He distinctively hears some kind of party inside. Music, voices, bursts of laughter. Between laughs, someone says, "I'll be back in a minute," and the detective barely has time to hide before the door opens and out comes a coffin.

11. Mysterious noises in the middle of the night. Like enormous and arrhythmic blows of a mace against the floor. Now and then these are accompanied by the crash of a piece of furniture or the sound of dishes

breaking. Hearing the sounds grow closer, one of the characters cracks open the door of his room. Terrified, he sees a huge rhinoceros walk calmly down the corridor.

12. They are saying that the thief will find a way into the castle despite all precautions. How it will happen no one knows. Nevertheless, every possible precaution has been taken. At that moment, a servant announces that downstairs, in the vestibule, two men have just carried in a large trunk. Everyone goes downstairs. One of them whispers: "Now we've got them—this isn't such a bright way to go about it." He pulls out a revolver and casually orders the two men to open the trunk. When the lid is raised, more than a hundred chirping, screeching birds fly out. After circling the room twice in a group, the whole flock disappears up the stairs toward the floors above.

13. A girl is seen reading in the solitude of the hall. Covering the floor is a vast carpet, thanks to which the girl doesn't hear the footfalls of the aforementioned rhinoceros as it approaches her. When its muzzle nearly grazes her arm, the beast grunts. The girl turns her head, and instead of being frightened she acts irritated and scolds the beast: "In here again? Go on, get out." With a kick she shoos it out of the room.

14. While the girl sleeps, a secret door to her room opens and a shadowy figure enters and approaches her bed. He takes what appears to be a dagger from his pocket. At her bedside, after kissing her cautiously, he cuts, with scissors that only looked like a knife, a lock of hair.

15. In a room, with four candles placed around it, is a coffin in which lies a very beautiful woman who might be the bride. As the protagonist draws near her, the corpse opens its eyes and says, "Would you mind leaving me in peace?"

16. In the corridor of the castle, a suit of armor gushes blood from its chest. The casque is open, and it's clear that there is no one inside. In fact, the blood is dripping from a crack in the ceiling. The observer goes up to the room above the crack. In the middle of the room lies the bleeding body of the lord of the castle. Hundreds of birds peck at the cadaver and fly about the room.

17. A tempest. An owl among dead leaves. Rain against a windowpane. Tempest music. Someone must leave the castle. He puts on his raincoat but once outside finds a serene evening. All the details that made up the tempest were fictitious. The music came from a phonograph. The rain against the window was just water leaking from a few flowerpots on the floor above. The owl is stuffed and sitting in the window of a display cabinet, etc.

18. A offers his hand to B as the two are introduced. Suddenly B screams and withdraws his hand from A's. All the fingers on A's right hand have been amputated.

19. The detective finds an excuse to leave the castle and later return in disguise, the better to carry on with his investigation. He comes back as an old peasant. Despite the perfection of his costume and beard, everyone recognizes him immediately. "How absurd. Why are you in disguise?" "That looks great. I almost didn't recognize you," another says, and so on. None of this should seem comic.

20. At a certain moment in the action, a small box comes into the hands of the young girl, who had spoken fearfully about it in earlier scenes. When she opens the box, the girl's face shows profound terror. She faints. The leading man arrives, and after helping the girl, he too sees what's in the box. His face changes; his eyes open wide. He closes the

box in horror. At that moment, something happens—a fire breaks out, for example—that will annihilate the two characters and the box, so that what was in it can never be known.

21. As a terrible punishment, a person is shackled in the castle dungeon, his arms extended and fastened to the wall. A small wound is inflicted on the palm of his hand, in which fly or beetle larvae are cultivated. Soon hundreds of worms seethe in his hand.

22. A scene of struggle. A grabs a knife and lunges at B. Then B steps back and pulls a sword from a suit of armor. Upon seeing this, A takes out a revolver. B flees. He reaches a cannon and fires a shot at A.

23. A woman with a magnificent head of blond hair flees her pursuer. She is caught as she runs through a door, which her pursuer slams on her hair.

*From the Spanish; the title is in English. Written in 1944?*

# Hallucinations about a Dead Hand

A man is quietly reading at his desk. It is about 11 P.M. Before him lies a thick open book.

Weird background music begins now.

We hear the cuckle of a rooster far away. Like an echo we hear the same cuckle closer, but with the soundtrack played in reverse. A fire is burning in the fireplace. Strange noises can be heard. One of them makes the man stare with fearful suspicion. It is as if a hand had brutally broken the strings of some musical instrument.

It is 11 P.M. We hear the chimes ringing the hour at the church tower, and as if by a reverberating echo, the same chimes are heard but now playing the sound in reverse.

The man looks to his right. He sees the rope of the bell of his room oscillating as if moved by a hand. Then he is truly alarmed and looks fearfully around him.

"Click, click, click."

(This sound is like the one that can be made by smashing the middle finger against the base of the thumb.)

"Click, click, click."

A book falls from the shelf. The logs in the fireplace crumble.

The man wipes the sweat from his forehead with his big handkerchief. Nervously he places it before him on the table.

"Click, click, click."

This time the noise comes from the table near the handkerchief. The man looks at it, truly scared.

He sees the handkerchief moving slowly. Its folds move like the petals of a carnivorous flower. (This shot and the following ones with the handkerchief and hand taken with slow-motion camera.)

Suddenly the most unusual and horrible face appears between the folds of the handkerchief, which frames the weird face like a sudarium.

The face has no forehead, and between the two inhuman minuscule black eyes, a big sharp, soft nose protrudes upon a mouth with no teeth and with only the lower jaw. This face slowly turns unexpectedly into a hand that begins to slide toward the scared man.

(This face is formed by a hand in which the middle finger makes the nose and the thumb the lower jaw. The eyes are two black points, like two small lead shots.)

The man gets up and steps back, while the hand goes on sliding.

(Always as we see the hand it has to slide and not walk, because then it could soon be associated with the representation of a common rat.)

When the hand reaches the edge of the table, it falls flat on the floor, making a noise like the one that can be made by an open palm striking a bulk of dough.

The hand remains for a moment inert, dull on the floor.

The man begins to react. His fear is being transformed into anger, but he still steps back as the hand begins again to go forward. The man makes up his mind. He searches in his pockets as if looking for a weapon. He has nothing. He looks around him to find something to annihilate his obstinate enemy.

Near him he sees a small brass statue supported by a heavy marble stand. Quickly the man throws away the statue and takes the stand vigorously in his arms, and with furious decision he drops it on the rampant hand. It is nearly smashed. Two or three fingers have remained outside the base of the stand. The man's eyes open with surprise.

Close-up. The stand is sliding in his direction. The hand carries it like a snail its shell.

He quickly kicks out the stand and, leaning over, takes the hand by its middle finger. Then the other fingers lamentably hang, soft and inarticulate like a glove.

The man goes toward the window, opens it, and throws the hand outside, but he has scarcely gotten rid of it when the hand, coming back as if pushed by an imaginary wind, smashes into his face with its palm open, again making the characteristic noise of a hand hitting dough.

The man grabs the hand again and throws it through the window, closing it immediately after. This time he is sure to have gotten rid of the hand.

Still panting, he goes back toward his desk, but suddenly his face contracts with repulsion and horror. He puts his hands on his chest and with his eyes wide open, he sees the fingers of the hand slowly coming out from his half-open shirt, and then the hand emerging from his *own* chest.

Mad with anger, he resolutely takes the mutilated organ and grasps it furiously with his own left hand while he takes a dagger with his right one. Then he goes to the table and places the dead hand on it.

Close-up. The two left hands, both the dead and the alive. The audience does not know which of these two hands is the dead one.

Close-up of the man, with a furious face, raising his right hand that holds the dagger and looking with hate toward the hands on the table. Then he drops the dagger. . . .*

Close-up of the two left hands. The dagger goes through one of them. Scream of pain. One of the hands is nailed by the dagger on the table. The other begins to slide. The man had pierced his own hand.

With decision he pulls out the dagger and stops the sliding hand with a single hit of the dagger, finally nailing the dead hand to the table.

THE END

Luis Buñuel
5642 Fountain Avenue
Hollywood (28), Calif.

*From a typescript in English, May 1944.*

*[The typescript continues with a phrase that is not clearly legible: "like a man who dabs"(?)—Trans.]

# Illegible, the Son of a Flute

A street in a tranquil neighborhood, with hardly any stores. People come and go. A uniformed policeman walks by, visibly agitated. It is easy to see that he is going through one of those critical moments in life that require radical solutions. He wipes his eyes with the back of his hand. When he reaches the corner, he suddenly takes his gun from the holster and fires a shot into the roof of his mouth. He collapses. A few curious people, half-stunned, half-alarmed, begin to form a circle around him. The attention of one man, about thirty-five years old, is drawn powerfully to the gun that the policeman still holds in his right hand. He stares at it, and the weapon comes into close-up. The passerby in question makes his way forcefully through the circle.

"Allow me; I am a doctor," he says.

He kneels down next to the policeman. He removes the gun from his hand and holds it in his own left hand while he takes the policeman's pulse. He opens the policeman's other hand, which clutches a crumpled photograph of a woman. Taking advantage of the curiosity aroused by the picture, he slips the gun into his pocket. He says, "There is nothing to be done. He's dead. I will call the Red Cross."

This is a pretext. We see him walk hurriedly through the streets and into a passageway. He goes up some stairs and stops before the door of an apartment. He inserts a key into the lock and tries in vain to open the door; it is bolted from the inside. Thinking that perhaps he is at the wrong door, he looks up to read a card, on which he finds his name:

LEANDRO VILLALOBOS. He then rings the bell and knocks repeatedly with his knuckles. A woman's voice replies from within.

"Who is it?"

"It's me."

When he utters the word "me," a loud noise can be heard, as if a large glass service had been shattered. Startled, he looks all around, as if trying to find the cause.

At this point the door is finally opened by a surprised woman with disheveled hair.

"Is that you, Leandro? . . . How come you're back so soon?"

"And you, why did you lock yourself in?"

"You know how fearful I am . . ."

He goes to his study, in which we see a very heavy desk with a wing-chair. A large armoire with two doors in which one or two people might fit perfectly. Bookshelves. Prominent on one of the walls is a large illustration of the human brain, which has been stuck with many small flags, just like those seen on military maps. There is also a mirror on the wall. In a corner of the room can be seen a large statue of Rodin's *Thinker*, whose head is covered by what appears to be the hood of a beauty-parlor dryer.

He glances at the poster of the brain, which resembles mountainous terrain. He reflects for a moment, as if thinking through some strategic operation, while his wife talks to him.

"What is wrong with you?"

"What do you mean? Nothing. That is to say, I think I have found the way to solve the problem."

"To earn enough money so we can live decently?"

"Bah! You know very well that for me there are more important things."

He has taken the gun from his pocket and placed it on the desk. She looks at him and at the gun with shock, then turns her gaze toward the armoire, visibly terror-stricken. Her fear grows as her husband walks to the armoire and opens one of its doors. He takes out a white shirt, and a skeleton can be seen hanging inside the armoire.

As he puts on the shirt he tells his wife, "Go on, get out."

"But what's the matter with you? You're scaring me. One would think you were about to commit a crime . . ."

"Don't be silly; I'm not going to kill myself. On the contrary. There is something I've wanted to know for a long time, something here, inside my head, that I am now about to find out . . . Leave me alone, I tell you . . ."

He pushes her gently toward the door, which he locks after her.

He then approaches Rodin's *Thinker*. He unplugs the dryer and carefully removes the hood. He sticks a tiny key into a lock in the statue's left ear and, after turning it, uses a cloth to carefully remove the top of the cranium, taking care not to burn himself. He pulls out a roasted dove whose shape recalls a brain. He cuts off a wing with a bit of the breast and eats it.

At the same time, he goes over to a small cabinet and takes out a bottle of water and a glass. He pours a little liquid into the glass and then drops in two tablets from a vial of Veronal. He stirs them in and drinks. The phone rings. He approaches the mirror and picks up a small receiver whose cable crosses the surface of the mirror such that when he looks into it, it seems as though the cable emerges from between his eyebrows. Although two voices are heard, his and another that sounds somewhat metallic and muffled, it is as if he were talking to himself. The dialogue will express, in as few words as possible, that the time has finally come to solve the problem that has so preoccupied him. This "idea," this truth that has been running through his head for some time without his being able to capture it, will now have to give itself up. The gun that has brought death to a policeman must surely have a special power. It is something like an irresistible magical instrument. Nevertheless, he is still not consciously aware of how it can be used. Something must be done, but he does not know what. It is not a matter of committing suicide or of shooting anyone else. He has come to the conclusion that he must give his subconscious an opportunity to manifest itself. Namely, he has decided to go to sleep with the gun in his hand so that whatever has to happen will happen. It is with this in mind that he has just taken the Veronal tablets.

When the conversation is over, he hangs up the receiver and sits down at the desk. He takes out a notepad. In red ink he crosses out his name on the letterhead: Leandro Villalobos, 27 Disillusion St. In its place he writes: *Illegible, the son of a flute.*

A commotion is heard in the street. He leans out the window. People are crowded together looking up at the eaves of the house across the street, from which another uniformed policeman is about to jump. The nervous spectators scold him and warn him to move away from the ledge. But the policeman ignores them and dives headfirst just as an ambulance is about to go by. He lands a few feet in front of the ambulance, which brakes and comes to a stop. The emergency team rushes out and collects the body. As they hoist it into the ambulance, the bodies of two other policemen can be seen inside.

"How awful!" says Illegible. "Truly it is now or never . . ."

With this he seems to mean that the day on which these strange events take place is exceptionally propitious for achieving his own aim. Perhaps in his thoughts a relation has been established between this attitude of the city's policemen and the disappearance of censorship in his psyche . . .

He sits back at his desk. He notices a blanket of dust on top of it. He traces a few lines with his finger and then mechanically writes "Avendaño" (a Spanish surname).

He says, "Avendaño? Why Avendaño? Who could Avendaño be? Could this have been my father's last name?" Judging by these words it seems that one of the reasons he is preoccupied is that he does not know his true identity, thus revealing that he had no parents.

The Veronal tablets have begun to take effect, and he falls asleep with the gun in his hand.

Once he is fast asleep, a sudden shot rings out. Illegible jumps, knocking over the table and chair, and falls to the floor, trapped beneath the furniture. The red ink spills onto his head. It looks as if he has committed suicide.

Loud knocks are heard at the door as his wife screams: "My God! Holiest Mother of God! Open the door, let me in!"

A door of the armoire opens slowly and the skull of the skeleton seen earlier cautiously emerges. A moment later the skull is withdrawn and the tousled head of the wife's lover appears. He looks at Illegible on the ground. Then he steps out from his hiding place, leaving the skull on top of the skeleton, and goes over to the door, letting in the woman who has continued to scream.

The lover says, "He's killed himself!"

"Poor thing . . . But what a scare—I thought he had killed you!"

They join hands and tell each other, "Thank God you made it out. What a close call!" "It's because I am me . . ."

When the word "me" is uttered, just as earlier there was the sound of glass breaking, now there is a very loud sound like that of chains . . .

Illegible, who has heard everything, groans and complains. He acts as if he were just waking up and says with difficulty: "Get this table off of me."

They do so. Illegible stands up gingerly.

"But aren't you dead?" his wife says.

"You are now about to find out."

He has blocked their way to the door, which he locks again with the key. After letting them know that he has heard everything, at gunpoint he makes them stand back to back. He takes a long cord from the curtains and begins to tie them together, arm to arm, hand to hand, leg to leg, foot to foot.

"Two bits to whoever can sit down first!" he says, while the woman cries and laments and the lover insults him.

"I bet you like to dance close to each other," Illegible tells them. "Let's see how you manage now . . ." He goes over to a radio that is on a small table and turns it on. He looks for dance music, which plays as he continues tying them at the waist, and so on.

The music is interrupted by an impassioned voice announcing that something extremely strange is happening in the city. No one knows why policemen are committing suicide. The oddest thing is that, as far as one can tell, each of the suicides was for personal reasons—some because of relationships, others because of trouble of various kinds: gambling debts, terminal illness, and so on. Eighty bodies have been recovered so far, and it is feared that those still alive are anxious and in turmoil.

Should they spot a policeman, citizens are advised to try to disarm him and not let him out of their sight, in order to prevent this inexplicable end . . .

Illegible says: "Now you see that today one can do whatever one likes with you without any worries."

"What is clear is that you are a frustrated policeman . . . You couldn't even succeed in killing yourself."

Illegible finishes tying them, wrapping the cord around their necks so that if one tries to get loose the other will be strangled. "Now we shall see," says Illegible, "who loves whom the most—which of you consents to be killed so that the other may live."

While the radio plays a solemn tune, Illegible gets ready to leave. He gathers his things. He opens the door, says goodbye to them, and locks it from the outside.

Now the lover is seen trying to free himself; in the process he strangles his mistress after a few feet of grotesque contortions. But he cannot manage to extricate himself and remains on the floor, tied to her cadaver. This has all been seen through the keyhole. But Illegible is not the one who sees it.

Illegible also locks the door to the stairs with a key. He goes out into the street. He ties the keys to a stone that he finds on the ground and upon passing a mailbox in the shape of the gaping maw of a lion, he tosses them in. They sound as if they were bouncing against the walls of a cave or a very deep well and finally make a little plop as if falling into water.

An uncommon effervescence reigns over the city on account of what has happened to the policemen. People come and go in a rush, while others huddle together to discuss the events. Some groups listen to the radios playing inside shops, whose owners, fearing evildoers, keep their metal grating half-closed. Illegible walks down the street and comes to a building that seems to be police headquarters. Two ambulances enter its courtyard, and as he walks by he sees strewn on the ground the corpses of countless policemen.

Instead of stopping, Illegible walks faster. After he has walked a couple more blocks, his attention is suddenly drawn to the presence of a young woman, about twenty years old, who is leaning against a door, indifferent to all that is going on around her. She cradles a large book, perhaps a music book, in her left arm. Her distracted attitude contrasts sharply with the agitation of everyone else. Illegible turns and looks at her. It seems as if several rays emanate from around her head, which in reality are part of an advertisement painted behind her. The most observant viewers should be able to sense that this female figure bears a certain relation to the Statue of Liberty.

Illegible walks back past the deeply absorbed woman. Finally he makes up his mind and approaches her.

He says jokingly, "Were you waiting for me?"

"Naturally."

"For a long time?"

"Anything is possible."

"For years?"

"And why not centuries?"

"I bet your name is Life."

"You lose. It's just Imprisonment."

"What are you studying?"

"Music."

"All right, come with me," Illegible says. "I have so much to tell you, but I'm in a hurry . . ."

He takes her by the hand and heads down the street again. A short while later we see them get out of a public vehicle, which leaves them at a park, through which they walk to a forest. They talk as they're walking. He tells her that tomorrow he will leave the city forever. He does not know where he will go, but it will be as far away as possible. He asks her to go with him. She seems quite willing.

"With you I could go to the end of the world."

Now well into the forest, they sit down on the grass among the trees. She asks if he would excuse her for a bit while she goes off into the thickets. Next we see her emerge naked from the waist up, covered with nothing more than a cloth in the same position as the one on the *Venus de Milo*. Fully illuminated by the setting sun, she walks with her eyes gazing into the infinite, as if in her sleep, and stops in front of him. He rises brusquely to his feet. After a moment of puzzlement, Illegible frowns. One would say he is deeply disappointed. He insults her, calls her a hussy, and so on.

"You deserve a beating . . . ," he says, as he helps her put on a coat.

She begins to cry inconsolably, so much so that Illegible has no choice but to go over and comfort her. He takes her hand and caresses it. He tries to joke with her, telling her that if she keeps crying like this they will drown in a sea of tears. On her wrist he sees a modest watch. He proposes that as a token of friendship they exchange watches. She agrees. He asks her if she lives far away. She tells him that she lives nowhere. Once again, he gets angry.

It is growing darker. She looks stealthily at him with a profound, nurturing gaze, the way a mother might look at her child in the most moving moments of life. It starts to drizzle. Night has fallen. Illegible suggests they return to the city. She goes along, naked beneath the coat. She leans on his shoulder. He realizes that she is having trouble walking.

"What's wrong? Are you tired?" he asks.

"I don't know. It's hard for me to walk."

The moonlight shines on her face. Illegible is surprised; one wouldn't think this was the same person. She seems ten years older. The light recedes, and her gait becomes more arduous. The moon illuminates her again, and Illegible finds her still older. It is now raining hard. He lights a match that the rain douses.

"But what is happening to you?"

"Nothing. I feel weak."

"One would say that darkness doesn't suit you, that it ages you."

"Who knows?" she replies.

He lights another match and holds it up to her face. He asks her if the light gives her any relief, and she says yes, and in fact it does seem to rejuvenate her a bit. They take shelter under a tree and sit down on a tree trunk. Illegible looks for something with which to build a fire, but everything around them is drenched. He takes some papers from his pocket and lights them. He calls out for help. No one answers. The papers burn and the fire goes out. When he lights the next match he sees that she has aged considerably. He burns everything he has on him—his identification papers, his cash . . . Now hardly any matches are left. Illegible is completely beside himself. The darkness returns. Her voice sounds cracked.

When she appears again, her teeth are missing. At one point her aging becomes extreme.

At that moment, as he holds her in his arms and lights the last match, she falters and cries out, between sobs, "Son, my son!"

Illegible is inexpressibly moved. All at once he has the feeling that the woman expiring in his arms is his mother, the mother he never had and who is now about to die . . . He holds her close to his heart, drinks in her breath.

"Mother! Mother!"

The woman's breathing slows, and little by little she dies in Illegible's arms. When he realizes she is dead, he lays her down gently on the tree trunk and goes away, shouting, "Mother! Mother!"

He returns shortly with a lantern he has found nearby. There is nothing in the place where he left the body. But at the foot of the trunk, on the other side, he sees a sack of wheat, as if it had fallen there, its contents flowing out through a large tear . . . With a touching naturalness, Illegible gets down on one knee and fills his pockets with this wheat, failing to notice that meanwhile She, now young again, is watching him from behind some branches, and that as he sets out saying to himself, "Mother! Mother!," she walks along behind him, accompanying him like a ghost.

Carrying out the plan of a trip that Illegible had announced to the woman who died in his arms, our character is seen on the steps of a train car as it slowly pulls out of the station. His suit is covered with dust. Passing alongside the tracks are several billboards with the name of the city in letters a foot high: *Villalobos*. Illegible carries a clothes brush in his hand with which he vigorously brushes himself, raising a cloud of dust from his suit that almost competes with the puffs of smoke from the locomotive. When no more dust comes from his suit, he starts on his shoes. Finally he throws the brush against one of the billboards that reads *Villalobos*, which makes a clanking sound, and enters the train car. He washes his hands and settles into an empty compartment.

A little later, a traveler somewhat older than Illegible enters the compartment. He carries a brand new suitcase of fine leather: luxurious luggage, worthy of a transatlantic passenger, which contrasts with the modest bearing of its owner. After carefully examining the space, he timidly says hello, places his suitcase on the rack, and sits down across from Illegible.

While landscapes gallop by out the window, the traveler begins to show signs of restlessness. He grows anxious, his expressions change. He seems to be gripped by sharp pains. His uneasiness becomes so obvious that Illegible starts to get nervous. He asks if he can be of any assistance. The traveler tells him that he does not feel well, but he doesn't think anyone can help him.

They strike up a conversation, but finally the man can no longer restrain himself. He breaks down and starts speaking rapidly. "Sir," he says, "I would give anything for you to believe me. I hope you don't think I'm crazy, though it may seem so. You have no idea what's happening. We are headed for disaster . . ."

Illegible looks at him with curiosity and some suspicion. Might he not be a madman who, taking advantage of the disappearance of the police, has escaped from an asylum? The traveler begins to tell his story.

"Believe me. My situation is such that you will soon understand the need I have to get this off my chest right now." The traveler's narrative is accompanied by the necessary images, which are seen on one side of the screen, as still shots, like the images of a magic lantern.

He says he was a modest office employee in an extremely modest office. [*Still shot.*] While walking along the boulevards during his lunch breaks, he always felt drawn to shops that specialized in travel items. One day an extremely fine suitcase caught his eye, behind which he saw a beautiful woman who was watching him and smiling. [*Still shot.*] He never saw the woman again. But after that day no more than twenty-four hours would pass before he had to go look at the suitcase again, so fearful was he that it would disappear. One day it finally happened. He felt as if his girlfriend had left him to sell herself . . .

But when he returned heartbroken to his modest apartment and entered his room, he found that the suitcase was there, at the foot of his bed . . . [*Still shot.*] How could this be? Who had sent it to him? He never was able to find out. A smartly dressed deliveryman, in a suit with braided trim, had come asking for him, for Avendaño, and had left it there . . .

Upon hearing the name *Avendaño*, Illegible reacts strongly. He remembers that this is the name he had unconsciously written on the table in his room the night before.

Visibly shaken, he asks, "Your name is Avendaño?"

"At your service."

The traveler goes on to say that no one in the store could account for it . . . A mystery. From then on the suitcase became for him an obsessive invitation to travel. He wasn't quite able to explain it. Sometimes he thought that the woman who had appeared next to the suitcase that first day was waiting for him somewhere, very far away . . . [*Still shot.*] In any event, he had to start saving his money so that one day he could take the train to the nearest beach. He absolutely had to see the sea. When it became possible to do it, he excitedly took his ticket, as if on a honeymoon, and sat down, like today, in a compartment. But not long after the train began to move, he felt ill. He thought at first that it was motion sickness. But his discomfort grew, turning into a pain that became more and more unbearable and seemed to come from his very bones.

"You can imagine how painful it was, since I thought I was about to die. But suddenly . . ." [*Stock shot of a violent derailing of cars, with the corresponding crashing noise.*] Avendaño goes to say that fortunately both he and his suitcase emerged unscathed, and his pain instantly went away. He chose to return to Villalobos, his point of departure, and did so without experiencing any discomfort.

As soon as he started to forget about the unpleasant mishap, he had no choice but to begin saving again. The suitcase signified for him the existence of something unspeakably marvelous . . . Every time he opened it, it seemed a certain music would drift out and transport him, together with an aroma of ripened tropical fruits.

Finally he set out on another trip, not without some apprehension. Unfortunately, everything repeated itself—the rabid, inexplicable pains, as if giving birth to who knows what, only to end in a train crash. [*Still shot.*] We see the crash of two trains whose locomotives are stacked one above the other. Over this image we hear Illegible's voice.

"It happened on July 18, 1936. I remember it perfectly, because I was supposed to have been on that train but was fortunate enough to miss it at the last minute."

"You were supposed to have been on that train?" Avendaño asks, intrigued.

"That's right."

"Well, you're lucky you weren't. Not a single passenger made it out safe and sound."

He, however, emerged from the terrible crash unharmed. The trip he is now taking is the third, and he is feeling the same precursory pains. The traveler asks Illegible for help.

"Please save me. Tell me what kind of cruel fate pursues me. Why are such beautiful promises transformed right before me into horrific cataclysms? Am I perhaps the cause of these accidents, or does my presence in them follow from other reasons I am not aware of? Save me. Tell me that you believe me, that you have compassion for me. Throw me off the train; perhaps that way you will avoid this frightful catastrophe, even worse than the two previous disasters, judging from these pains, which are more acute this time than they were before."

Illegible tries to calm him. But there are moments when he thinks it is all a bad joke, assuming the man is not crazy. Sometimes he answers him sharply, suspiciously. Furthermore, with all that has happened to him since the previous night, it's getting to be too much. He thought he was leaving that behind him, and here the arbitrary descends on him again. He will end up insane, for surely no one's nerves can take all this.

Avendaño does not give up, insisting each time with more urgency. In his distress, Illegible thinks that maybe there is something inside the mysterious suitcase that will shed light on the traveler and his strange tales. He asks Avendaño if he may check the suitcase to see what is in it. Avendaño refuses: "What is the point?" Illegible insists, but Avendaño will not give in. His refusal exasperates Illegible, who is getting more and more nervous. Avendaño warns Illegible of the imminence of the catastrophe; he feels it in the magnitude of his pains. Illegible cannot stop himself and takes the suitcase down from the rack. Avendaño jumps on him. Jealousy? They engage in a violent struggle, in which he even tries to bite Illegible. As they roll on the floor, holding on tightly to each other, the catastrophe strikes. The train goes off a cliff to the bottom of a ravine. On top of the smoking wreck of train cars, we see the suitcase tumble. When it comes to a stop it opens, and a dove flies out and away. The suitcase is then engulfed in flames as Avendaño and Illegible helplessly look on, having managed to escape intact through the splintered and twisted steel of the wreckage.

Meanwhile moans and heartrending screams for help can be heard, which no one heeds. We see smashed and dismembered limbs, pools of blood, and so on. The two survivors leave the scene of the disaster and walk toward a slope across from it. Avendaño is a bit shaken; Illegible helps him walk, putting one of Avendaño's arms over his neck. He asks him if he feels all right.

Avendaño answers, "It's nothing, I feel a little startled, but that will soon pass . . ."

After a pause, while they walk, Illegible comments, "So this was the third time?"

"Did I not try to tell you that?"

"And the dove, why did you have that dove?"

"But I never put it there; I only packed some white underwear . . ."

They have sat down on the grass. Avendaño, at first leaning on his side, ends up lying down. Illegible sees him there with his eyes closed, so pale . . . Has he passed out? He feels concerned about him; by starting that fight, didn't he perhaps save his life? He speaks to him, but there is no answer. He shakes him; he fans him with his hand. He tries to take his pulse, but he can't seem to find it. He shakes him harder. In vain. Finally he puts his ear to Avendaño's heart. He must hear something unusual . . . Indeed: we hear the beats of his heart amplified like the firing of a machine gun. Then the din of a violent battle. Then just the machine gun again, whose shots follow an unexpected rhythm, which soon is recognized as Morse code. *Tac, tac-tac–tac–tac-tac tac*, etc.

Illegible takes a pencil and paper and begins to transcribe the sounds in letters. We see him write: *"Finally the long-awaited hour is near . . . Already the other shore is beginning to trace future footsteps in the sand . . . Hurry, hurry . . . If not, you will be late to the creation of the world . . ."*

"Who are you talking to?" Illegible asks.

"To you who can hear me," the Morse code answers.

"But who am I?"

"You? Who else could you be? Illegible . . . The Son of a Flute . . ." Nothing more is heard. The heart resumes its natural rhythm in the face of Illegible's perplexity. Avendaño's face returns to normal. Illegible helps him up and leans him against a tree trunk. Once this is done, Illegible sets out for a walk, going back and forth with his hands behind his back, agitated. From the wreckage of the train we see a body emerge and head toward them. It is a very strange character. He is a hunchback, and it appears his limbs do not match well with one another, to the extent that Illegible, stopping as he passes by, has the impression that perhaps he has just been assembled from the remains of several dismembered passengers. He is also characterized by the various gadgets he has on him: a hearing aid in the latest style; a walkie-talkie, a new model with an antenna that goes well past his head; a first-class orthopedic leg, which can be glimpsed through his shredded pants. As he walks he speaks on his walkie-talkie.

"Hello, hello . . . The accident has occurred in the precise place. I will arrive as we agreed at noon the day after tomorrow . . . I hope all will be ready onboard so that we can sail immediately . . ."

"Have you noticed what a strange character that is?" asks Avendaño.

"Yes, I had the absurd impression that he had just been formed from the remains of those who perished in the wreckage. But it must be that I'm going nuts . . ." Illegible replies, as he keeps walking.

The strange character has just come up to them.

"Hello partners," he says cheerfully. "You folks seem a little distraught. Has something awful happened to you?"

"Hello," Illegible responds curtly, as he keeps walking.

"Do you folks have any idea how to get out of here?"

"Not the remotest idea," Avendaño answers.

The newcomer picks up the paper on which Illegible had deciphered the Morse code and inspects it with curiosity.

"Which one of you is Illegible, the Son of a Flute?" he asks.

"At your service," answers Illegible, after a moment's hesitation.

"And why do they call you that?"

"Do you really want to know?" Illegible answers, annoyed.

"Why not?"

Illegible hesitates again. In his agitated state he looks as if he is about to tell the man to take a hike. But in the end he explains.

"Because I was a foundling. To show that my name was not known, that in truth I did not have a name, my fellow students at university called me 'Illegible.' On one occasion one of them, as an insult, called me 'The Son of a Flute'—hence the name."

"But why are you fretting? Because you don't have a mother? . . . Bah! . . . What would you say if I told you that I had just been formed from the remains of various passengers put together in a single body? You wouldn't believe me, would you? And what if I told you my name was Left Cheek?"

"What did you say?" interrupts Illegible aggressively, standing in front of him.

"Left Cheek . . ."

Unable to restrain himself, Illegible gives him a big slap in the face. The newcomer looks at him with rage and reaches in his back pocket.

Avendaño leaps to his feet to stop Cheek, telling him, "Forgive him, he's a bit overexcited . . ."

Cheek takes out not a revolver but a vibrator, with which he massages the cheek that was just slapped, saying, "It was nothing."

"And what do you have there?" Illegible asks, still in an aggressive tone, as he points to Cheek's hump.

"What do you think I have? The storage batteries . . . But let's change the subject. Where were you two headed?"

"We were headed for catastrophe, and now we have arrived," Avendaño replies.

"In that case, why don't you come with me? We'll go on foot for now."

Swayed by Cheek's cold-blooded attitude and tone, they set forth. He tells them he has a small sailboat with a crew of four awaiting him at Cape Finisterre, ready to depart as soon as he arrives. There are, according to him, certain basic problems within man's social life that cannot be solved in the overpopulated areas of our contemporary world. For that reason he got the idea of looking for the island that men have talked about from time immemorial, that island that eludes navigators, having a life of its own, and moves from one place to another throughout the oceans and perhaps submerges itself in them like a whale. There in that floating and movable dimension, in that virgin land, is where the realities that preoccupy him can be born . . . It is necessary to encounter it as if by chance, turning oneself into bait so that the island may come to them of its own accord. Illegible and Avendaño are invited to join the expedition. Since neither has any worldly ties, they accept. Cheek congratulates them. He thinks they will make excellent bait, seeing as they are survivors of such a catastrophe. Through his walkie-talkie he contacts the boat to announce that he will be bringing two friends.

They have come to the road. We see them leaving from behind. In the distance we hear a shepherd's flute as he watches over his flock. We see him with six lambs around him, in much the way as the Good Shepherd is seen in the mosaic over the tomb of Galla Placidia in Ravenna.

We are at high sea. We see our three characters in a two-mast sailboat, about sixty-five feet in length, called the *Insatiable*. Four sailors travel with them. Some are in their shirtsleeves, others are bare-chested; all are barefoot and browned by the sun. Their long beards tell us that they have been at sea for many weeks.

One afternoon, while the sea is a bit choppy and a few black clouds are seen in the sky, as one of the travelers remarks with apprehension, one of the crew screams twice from the top of the mast. They cannot really make out what he is saying. It sounds like "Land to port!" . . . but perhaps he is screaming, "She's to port!"

Everyone gets nervous. No one can see anything, but they think that what the watchman has seen may be the famous island they're searching for.

Finally they see floating not far from the boat the nubile and naked body of a beautiful woman. Her perfect breasts emerge from the waters surrounded by sea foam. Her eyes are closed and her lips glisten, though she shows no signs of life . . .

"Could this be the isle?" says one of the sailors.

"Who knows!" Cheek answers. "For now I'll bet you anything it's not America."

They decide to bring her on board. The young woman is identical to the one who died in Illegible's arms, possibly the same. She may even be the same woman the policeman in the beginning of the story killed himself for, the same one Avendaño saw one day in the luggage store.

"No one is to touch her," Cheek decides.

The seven of them contemplate her, disturbed, each in his own way. Her nudity makes them uneasy. They cannot understand how she could be there. They lift her out in a net and place her carefully on the deck. Illegible is deeply moved. He hangs back from the group a bit and he starts to play the flute again very low, as if playing for himself.

Since the sea is choppy and it is getting dark, they decide to bring the young woman into the crew's chamber. Several men carry her in using the net and place her on the center table. They smoke, drink, and discuss. What is certain is that no one knows if she really drowned or if she is alive. One insists he saw her breathe, but the others assure him it must have been the waves. Two groups are formed: those who claim she is alive and those who maintain she is dead. If only they could touch her . . . But it is not allowed.

Illegible keeps playing his flute in a corner. Soon one of the sailors begins to hum the melody mechanically. Avendaño does so in turn, and one after another the voices join in, finally forming a chorus. The song they intone is deep and moving. It is a plainsong hymn that resonates profoundly with the sound of the tempest that has unleashed itself outside and seems to serve as an accompaniment.

There is a stormy northwest wind. The boat sways strongly. Objects move about or fall down. Lamps swing. Only the woman does not move, seemingly bolted to the table. The boat creaks alarmingly. The watchman, who has entered from time to time to warn them that the situation was worsening, now screams with terror that the mast has broken and things look very serious. Avendaño draws close to the young woman's feet and with tears in his eyes addresses her in a low, moving voice.

"I recognized you right from the start . . . I thought you were going to smile at me again . . . They say you are dead . . . What do they know! . . . But it is all the same, because I am going to instill my life into you . . . to reunite myself with you forever . . ."

We see Avendaño take the revolver from Illegible's coat, which hangs on a nail. At that moment we hear Cheek, who must have been arguing, say in a stentorian voice, while beating his chest with the palm of his hand, "Me, me, me!"

Simultaneously we hear a detonation. It seems that Avendaño has shot himself in the head.

At that moment everything comes falling down, as if the boat had crashed against a reef. The confusion is indescribable. All the lights go out, and even the body of the woman falls to the floor. Illegible, who has been thrown into a corner, suddenly finds himself next to the woman's naked body. She throws her arms around him and kisses him passionately on the mouth. He opens his hands and they are full of white feathers, as water and foam burst in and flood the chamber.

A deserted beach. We see Illegible sprawled on the sand, dressed as he was in the beginning but now barefoot. We get the impression that the shipwreck has just taken place. Illegible begins to come to. He sits up. He appears to be searching his memory. He observes his surroundings. He scans the empty horizon. He looks at his watch; it has stopped. He winds it. He instinctively looks up at the sun, which has reached its zenith. The light comes down at such a straight angle that neither he nor any of the objects that surround him cast a shadow. Seeing this, he sets his watch to noon. He shouts through cupped hands, but no one answers.

Not far from where the waves reach the shore, he sees something that catches his attention. It is a human footprint in the sand, only one—a right foot—with no trace of any other footsteps that would have led someone there.

He remembers the words he heard in Morse code in Avendaño's heartbeat. He goes up to the footprint and he presses his left foot next to it. The two footprints seem to have been made by the same person. He says out loud, *"Already the other shore is beginning to trace future footsteps in the sand . . . Hurry, hurry . . . If not, you will be late to the creation of the world."*

To see if the first footprint matches his, he places his right foot in it, and at that very instant another left and another right footprint appear all by themselves in the sand before him, and he puts his feet in each one. Footprints continue to appear spontaneously before him, eventually leading him to a place where a cavity has been made in the sand in the shape of a woman's body with outstretched arms. It looks like a very recent imprint. With excitement and joy, Illegible throws himself onto the imprint, hugging and kissing the sand.

When he gets up, his suit and face covered with wet sand, he sees Avendaño walking toward him, showing signs of happiness. They strike up a conversation in which Avendaño, who expresses himself in archaic language, addresses Illegible as Your Honor. He does not understand anything Illegible says about the shipwreck and the body of the young woman for whom he had committed suicide. His personal memories are very different. He thinks he is in the year 1942 and that the ship in which he sailed has sunk on an expedition to the Azores. This archipelago has nothing to do with the island that according to Illegible they had set off to find and which Avendaño knows nothing at all about.

Avendaño explains the scar on his temple, which does look quite old, in a way that bears no relation to the gunshot that Illegible remembers. Illegible once again begins to feel this is all a bad joke, that Avendaño is a lousy comedian who is putting him on.

"If Your Honor does not trust me, we must ask the man there who fishes among the rocks," says Avendaño.

Sure enough, Illegible sees a man in the distance whose silhouette unmistakably reminds him of Cheek, who is sitting on the seashore among some rocks with a fishing rod in his hands. They talk as they come near him. Cheek holds the rod with both hands, and instead of looking at the sea he gazes off into infinity, lost in his reverie, completely entranced.

Illegible approaches him and grabs the rod to shake it. But as soon as his hand touches the rod, an astonishingly profound music rings forth. Illegible pulls his hand away as if he had touched an electrical wire, and the music stops. He repeats the game twice more, with the same results. He and Avendaño exchange their impressions, as if they were fishing, and decide to imitate him. They look among the rocks for something that may resemble a rod or a pole. They find some twisted sticks, onto which they attach the gear. The moment the fishing line makes contact with the waves, a stirring symphony resounds, played by unrecognizable instruments that vibrate with the grandiosity of cosmic harmonies.

After a moment Cheek comes to, and with the music somewhat muted in the background, the three start a surprising conversation.

Illegible has noticed that there seems to be no clear correlation between the motion of his watch and that of the sun. The sun has only moved slightly from where it was when he first looked up at it, whereas the hands on his watch indicate that five and a half hours have gone by. It all gets even more complicated when he realizes that Cheek's memories do not coincide with either his or Avendaño's, because Cheek also speaks of a shipwreck, but one that took place in 1987.

Illegible turns the conversation to the following topics: Might not this beach on which they find themselves, and which no one can tell them anything about, belong to the famous island that they set off to find, on which a different dimension must exist? And might not the whole story of the shipwreck and the naked woman simply be the island's way of running them aground and taking them over? Since this island sails, perhaps at great speed, that might explain why the sun's motion is so much slower than that of his watch, unless his watch is broken.

On the other hand, might they even not be on Earth—which would explain why the sun moves more slowly—but on the planet Venus, for example, having died in the shipwreck and gone to the otherworld?

But above all there is doubt: Are they alive? Are they dead? Are they in another kind of time or perhaps in eternity?

They leave such profound topics to talk about more immediately practical concerns. It seems they are on a deserted beach on a lost island, and they need to fend for themselves, settling in like Robinson Crusoes. First they need to build a cabin for shelter and find something they can eat. We see them making a hut out of branches, but since they lack nails and ropes it is clear that their construction will not withstand the wind. They agree to go back to the sea, whose obligation is to provide the shipwrecked with remnants of the ship so they may be able to set themselves up. They find absolutely nothing. Illegible then tells them, "Let me sleep. You will see how the sea will bring us the things I dream of."

Which is exactly what happens. Illegible lies down on the sand, and while he sleeps, we see a double leave his body, stand up, and start walking, motioning Avendaño and Cheek to follow him. He goes toward a place where one can spot something floating near the seashore, a kind of wooden box. They go closer and see that it's a coffin.

Avendaño starts laughing, while Cheek looks at him with visible apprehension. Following Illegible's signals, the two of them push it to the shore and open it. Out comes a fish the size of a man, some sort of shark, which begins to leap about until it goes back into sea.

"Well, at least we still have the planks and the nails," says Avendaño. Illegible starts walking again to another place, where one can make out a type of large crate, similar to the ones used to transport theater sets. They go up to it and try to maneuver it but say it is too heavy. They cannot move it. But they take advantage of the force of the waves, which push it ashore, while Avendaño and Cheek secure it with large stones to keep the ebb tide from pulling it back to sea.

"What the hell could this be?" Avendaño asks himself.

They watch as the lid of the box opens by itself. Inside it there appear more than a few characters, arranged one over the other like toys, who immediately begin to stir and come out onto the beach in a type of procession. The first ones out, in groups of three, are twelve Franciscan friars with long beards, who make up a musical band. Each one plays a wind or percussion instrument, but oddly enough, no matter how hard one sees them blow into the trumpets and trombones, beat on the drum, and hit the cymbals, not a single sound is heard. What can be heard, however, is Avendaño's voice: "How discreet are the sons of Saint Francis."

After the friars, the characters from the drama *Life Is a Dream* by Calderón de la Barca step out and likewise file away in formation. We see among them King Basilio; Segismundo dressed in animal skins and restrained by a long chain attached to his hands; Estrella, etc. All of them have empty eye sockets.

As they come out of the box and proceed on the beach behind the Franciscans, heading toward a small hill that rises on the other side of the sea, the following verses from *Life Is a Dream* are heard, recited in a deep voice that resonates as if from a crypt:

And having more soul,
have I less liberty?

The voice gives way to the sound of the waves, whipped by the wind, which break on the beach. After a moment the voice sounds again:

And I, with better instincts,
have I less liberty?

The voice falls silent again and the ocean is heard, until the voice comes back:

And I with greater freedom of choice,
have I less liberty?

The same sound game repeats itself as the procession moves farther from the sea:

And having more life,
have I less liberty?

The procession has receded from the beach and makes its way up the hill while the three castaways, Cheek, Avendaño, and the shadow of Illegible, start walking behind them, as if drawn by an invincible force. In a matter of moments we see Illegible's sleeping body get up and walk with the somnambulistic motion of a mechanical doll, and then start running with all his might. He catches up to his double and unites with him, acquiring his total consistency, and awakes.

This last maneuver has made Illegible and Avendaño fall behind, while Cheek has kept up with the friars and the dramatic characters who are about to disappear over the hill. When Cheek reaches the summit he finds that the procession has vanished, while in the middle distance he sees a huge beach unfold, as packed with people as the beach of Coney Island in its heyday. [*Stock shot of Coney Island.*]

Cheek's face transforms in enthusiasm at the sight of such a spectacle, while we hear lines from Calderón that began to be recited the moment he reached the summit:

What is life? A frenzy.
What is life? An illusion.
A shadow, a fiction.
And the greatest good is small:
All of life is a dream,
And dreams are but dreams.

In his ebullient enthusiasm, Cheek turns to his companions to urge them with gestures and voice to join him. And they do so. When they arrive at the summit, Cheek jubilantly shows them the spectacle.

But when Illegible and Avendaño look toward the place Cheek indicates, they see nothing but an unending desert, scattered with a few small cactuses and some very large ones.

"For a sterile landscape, it's not bad," Illegible says.

"What do you mean, a sterile landscape? And that immense beach bustling with people, full of humanity and richness . . . ? Or do you think such a massive gathering could take place in a poor spot?"

Illegible and Avendaño look stealthily at each other and use gestures to indicate that Cheek is delirious. They, in effect, see nothing but a desert like that of the southwestern United States or northern Mexico.

Cheek invites them to run to the beach, but Illegible and Avendaño take it as a joke. Very excited, Cheek finally tells them, "Well, all right, you can stay there." And he springs forward, soon to be hidden behind a giant cactus.

In no hurry, Avendaño and Illegible set out philosophically. When they reach the cactus, they don't see Cheek anywhere. They call out to him, they keep looking for him. Nothing.

"The earth swallowed him up," says Illegible.

"And now what do we do?" asks Avendaño.

Illegible sits on the ground to think and starts playing with the sand. A little later, Avendaño sits down as well, but just as his backside touches the ground, he cries out in pain: "Ouch!"

"What's wrong?"

"Someone has stuck me with a halberd," Avendaño answers while rubbing the sore spot.

"A halberd is what you deserve," responds Illegible laughing. "All this fuss over a cactus needle!"

"Sure, a needle," says Avendaño, after scratching around in the sand. "There is a damn metal point here. Look . . ."

He tries to remove the object he has unearthed, but he can't. He digs furiously until he finds that behind the point is a large metal object. Illegible sets to work with him.

We see them both labor intensely, using sticks they find nearby. They rest from time to time, wiping their sweat. They have just discovered a big statue of liberty, which with superhuman effort they manage to pull out and stand next to the cactus. This cactus is reminiscent of a skyscraper. The said statue is missing its right arm with the torch and part of its left arm; some of the rays on its crown are bent. It is corroded, as if it has been buried there for centuries. Next to it have appeared a series of objects from our time, the very ones that Cheek threw out to sea when the boat set sail. All the objects are rusted and give the impression of something extremely ancient.

"There must have been an immense city here, with very advanced technicians. Perhaps this is where the famous civilization of Atlantis was. This whole desert must be full of ruins . . . ," says Illegible.

The statue is lit by the setting sun, almost horizontally, casting a tremendously long shadow.

While they rest for a moment, commenting about the events, they hear to their right the neigh of a horse followed by a formidable bray. They both get up at the same time and run toward where the noise came from. Soon they see a skinny horse and a donkey rubbing their noses together.

The presence of those animals fills them with excitement. Illegible mounts the horse immediately and says, "Didn't I say you deserved a packsaddle?"*

Avendaño in turn jumps on the donkey, and both animals, as if obeying an order and without anyone spurring them, start walking. It is getting dark.

We see them go along, wrapped in shadow, led by the animals' instinct. Night falls. They doze off on their mounts. It appears that they spend the whole night on the move.

We see the sunrise. As the sun comes over a hillock, the animals stop brusquely before a post placed in the middle of the desert, topped with a sign like those set to mark a border. The sign reads, "Columbia."

Avendaño, who just woke up, yells at his companion, "Wake up, it's time! Look at the beautiful light of this new day's sun."

Illegible rubs his eyes. He reads the sign. He contemplates the desert.

Next to the post runs a trickle of water. They get down from their mounts, drink, and perform their ablutions. They comment that an inhabited or habitable land must begin around here.

They climb back on their animals and set out across the border. Then

---

*[Illegible puns on *alabarda* (halberd) and *albarda* (packsaddle).—Trans.]

we see that through the holes in Illegible's pocket grains of wheat pour from his jacket, ever more numerous, and fall to the ground. A little later, Avendaño turns to see how far they have traveled and is astonished to find that a row of wheat blades has been growing behind them. He tells Illegible, who is amazed and puts his hands into his pockets filled with grain. With the happiness of a child he scatters some of this wheat on the ground, and it is not long before we see it sprout . . .

"But what kind of a desert is this, with such soil?" says Illegible. "Take some," he says to Avendaño, inviting him to stick his hands in his pockets. He does so.

The two begin throwing wheat right and left, not as sowers would, but more like those who feed birds. They go from right to left and soon find themselves surrounded by an incipient wheatfield. Illegible, who has split off to the left while his companion has gone to the right, turns and is suddenly in front of a hillock, with the sun directly before him illuminating it. He sees something that surprises him. In the sky the shape of a woman is thrown into relief, something like an immense statue of the *Venus de Milo* with both her arms complete, the right one raised like that of the Statue of Liberty. She seems to have the sphere of the sun in her hand as a torch. This woman is the very same one who, illuminated by the setting sun, had shown herself naked to him in the forest . . .

Illegible shouts out loudly, "A miracle! A miracle! . . ."

Avendaño arrives on his donkey. Illegible turns to him and points to the vision, repeating, "A miracle!"

But as he looks again at the sun, the woman is no longer to be seen; instead there is a windmill with great sails, like the famous ones from La Mancha. Not without disappointment he then exclaims, "Oh, no . . . This time it's a windmill."

*From the Spanish. Written in 1947, based on the lost, unfinished original of 1927–28 by Juan Larrea and Luis Buñuel.*

# Agon

(Swansong)

*Interior: Norma's cell. Daytime.*

In her cell, brightly illuminated, Norma sits on her bed, covering her face with her hands and shouting.

*Norma*
Turn it off! Turn off that light!

She tumbles onto the floor and manages to slide under the bed. The light becomes less intense. Norma remains under the bed with her hands covering her face.

Suddenly the light goes out. Norma, surprised, raises her head slightly and looks down.

She sees part of the firmament; it's nighttime. Several planets can be clearly seen: Jupiter, Saturn and its rings, and a few distant galaxies that seem well defined and near.

We hear bells in the distance and birds singing.

Norma looks at the firmament, which seems to be under her head.

Now we can also hear the familiar sounds of the street: cars, horns, the footsteps of passersby.

Norma slides out of her hiding place, struggles to stand up, and staggers toward the cell's window.

The window is open. It lets in a ray of moonlight. She takes a breath, listens, and watches. A slight smile illuminates her face. She seems reassured.

She approaches the ray of moonlight and enters its soft glow.

Her flowing hair is suddenly covered with a light, white foam. Norma runs her fingers through her hair, as if she were washing it. Then she kneels in the bright moonlight and rinses her hair.

The moonlight turns into water. Her hair is dripping. She tries to drink the water that trickles down her face, but it is mixed with soapy foam. It's undrinkable. Norma spits it out with a grimace.

She throws her hair back, while her gaze is gently drawn toward the open window.

Two or three dozens moths—*sphynx*—flutter into the cell. Her gaze follows them. One lands on her hand. She brings the moth up to her eyes and examines it.

It is one of those moths that has a skull drawn on its thorax.

It also has on a minuscule headdress reminiscent of a bishop's miter. Between its legs it holds a small coiled metallic object that resembles a crosier.

Norma looks at it intensely, then raises her eyes.

She sees Archbishop Soldevilla, who has just entered her cell.

The archbishop is dressed in full priestly regalia, his crosier in hand. His bloodied body bears the fresh marks of the assassin's bullets.

He walks slowly, as if in slow motion. Apparently very tired, he goes to sit on the edge of the bed.

Norma, following him with her eyes, inquires:

*Norma*
What are you doing here, sir?

He looks at her before answering.

*Archbishop*
I've come to announce your death. You'll die in the next hour.

He is silent for a moment, then sadly continues.

*Archbishop*
You don't know the Second Coming of Christ is near?

*Norma*
Give me something to drink.

*Archbishop*
I'm thirsty too. But all the chalices in the world have turned into ink-wells.

He turns to the young girl.

*Archbishop*
Have you read today's stock market quotes?

*Norma*
No.

*Archbishop*
You haven't seen the interest on coal?

*Norma*
What?

*Archbishop*
The interest on coal. The coalinterest.

*Norma*
No.

*Archbishop*
Listen to me.

He opens the prayer book in his hand and looks for a page. The pages of the prayer book have never been cut open. He takes a paper knife out of his pocket and cuts them open. Then he reads:

*Archbishop*
"The cock barks on Mount Palatino.
I dreamt I stole a lemon from the pope's garden.
And that the pope chased me down the halls of the Vatican . . ."
Norma breaks in.

*Norma*
Get out of here.

The archbishop closes the book, stands up with difficulty, and, leaning on his crosier, moves toward the cell door. Before leaving, he turns to the young woman and says:

*Archbishop*
Think about your stockings.

She looks at her legs with surprise. At that moment the archbishop raises his right hand to bless her. As he does so, drops of blood splatter her face. Finally he leaves. The light abruptly returns to the cell. It is very bright, unbearable. Norma is alone. She cries.

•   •   •

*These are the final shots of the script:*

*Interior: music hall. Daytime.*
A man interrupts the show to say:

*Announcer*
Ladies and Gentlemen, the government has just issued the following bulletin, which I must read to you. Today a hydrogen bomb destroyed the city of Jerusalem and all the surrounding region. It is still not known who is responsible for the explosion. The USSR has not issued any state-

ment. NATO has been mobilized. The U.S. Sixth Fleet is heading to the area. The president of the Republic asks that all citizens calmly return home and confidently await further developments.

*Exterior: avenue. Daytime.*

The avenue in front of the music hall. Everyone, in a great state of confusion, exits the hall and jumps into taxicabs and buses.

We hear tanks and military trucks rolling down the avenue with their cannons pointing to the sky.

*Interior: cave. Nighttime.*

It's late, around three in the morning. A group of activists are meeting. They have just written a communiqué. Abel picks up the page and slowly reads the text to his comrades.

*Abel*

"To the President of the Republic:

"We hereby inform you that the group Revolutionary Action has dissolved. Our actions have become insignificant by comparison to the infinitely more powerful actions of the imperialists. Our ultimatum has been nullified. You will find our modest atomic bomb in a barge anchored across from the Louvre.

"We're going home. We'll be mobilized if it's not too late. We promise you then, if the opportunity arises to do so with impunity, we shall liquidate our officers by shooting them in the back."

*Exterior: sky. Daytime.*

The sky is dark and threatening.

The mushroom-shaped atomic blast looms ominously in the sky.

The clouds that crown the mushroom slowly dissipate.

An imprecise silhouette appears above the clouds.

This silhouette, which rests at the top of the mushroom, moves toward us. We recognize Christ, motionless, with his right hand raised.

He approaches little by little, in a halo of darkening clouds.

His eyes are empty sockets.

THE END

*From the Spanish. N.d.*

BUÑUEL ON BUÑUEL

# *Land without Bread*

Before screening the film that is the object of this gathering, I would like to say a few words about certain aspects of the land you are about to visit that are either not in the film or reflected there only briefly.

My aim in making this film was to objectively transcribe the facts offered by reality without any interpretation, less still any invention. I went with my friends to this incredible region, attracted by its intense drama, its terrible poetry. The little I knew of it through my reading had moved me; for centuries human beings had struggled there against a hostile environment, and without the least hope of ever gaining the upper hand. Travelers and geographers alike have deemed the place uninhabitable.

And yet the climate is mild, water is abundant, and vegetation spreads out in all directions. But the climate, the water, the vegetation, the earth, all seem to want to strangle human life rather than promote it. Though the bees make honey, the honey is too bitter to eat. Though the waters are pure, their very purity makes them pernicious, for they are devoid of essential mineral salts. Instead, they are the breeding ground for the dreadful anopheline mosquito. All the region's inhabitants have malaria.

I will now give the name of this region. It is called Las Hurdes and is located in eastern Spain, near the Portuguese border.

Until very recently Las Hurdes was cut off from the rest of the world by tall, labyrinthine mountains, accessible only to mountain climbers and deprived of normal human contact. There were no means of communication either to the outside or between towns inside the region. The first condition required for men to build a road is that it must lead

somewhere. Well, then: Las Hurdes doesn't lead anywhere. It's an iso-
lated land, on the margin of all human solicitude. It is not just hostile to
man; it rebels even against his passing.

Today a road cuts across the lower part of the region. Doctors have
been sent in, schools have been opened. But the towns higher up remain
as isolated as ever.

As an example of just how extreme the isolation is even between the
villages of Las Hurdes, consider the case of one of its inhabitants, who
told us that for nearly twenty years he had not seen a daughter of his
who had married into a neighboring village. The two villages were little
more than six miles apart. But to visit her would take many hours walk-
ing through thick brush along steep paths, and the people of Las Hur-
des must devote all their time, all their energy to arduous daily work on
land that scarcely provides them with bread.

Las Hurdes was unknown to most Spaniards until 1922. At that time
public attention was briefly drawn there following a trip to the region by
the former king of Spain, Alfonso XIII. It was said at once that the exis-
tence of such a region was the shame of Spain. Personally, I don't think
so. The problem of Las Hurdes is so profound, so mysterious that it es-
capes a simple government pronouncement. Our great Spaniard Una-
muno once said, perhaps paradoxically, that Las Hurdes is the glory
rather than the shame of Spain. Isn't it both admirable and pathetic, this
incessant fight by a handful of men who attempt to survive, working
hour after hour, century after century, without ever once losing heart in
their enterprise? And what if the existence of such a state of affairs were
indeed the shame of Spain? Let the country that is completely free of
social shame cast the first stone.

The first historical document we are aware of concerning the exis-
tence of Las Hurdes appeared in the sixteenth century in the form of a
comedy written by the prince of Spanish geniuses, Lope de Vega. The au-
thor had never visited Las Hurdes but had heard it spoken of as a primi-
tive, Arcadian land. It's curious that the discovery of this region by the

Spanish coincided with the discovery of America. The eternal contradiction of the Spanish genius: it discovers heaven and hell simultaneously.

It is thought that the first inhabitants of Las Hurdes settled there at the beginning of the sixteenth century. They were Jews who were fleeing the persecution of the Catholic monarchy and sought refuge in that lost land. The population subsequently grew with the arrival of a number of outlaws likewise running from the harshness of justice. In the centuries that followed, visitors were extremely rare in this land where human life had so incredibly established itself.

This introduction would grow too long if we were to recount the varied and "ingenious" methods by which nature infused with new blood the veins of the inhabitants of Las Hurdes, thus avoiding their total degeneration. I believe that the film addresses some of this.

Nor is this the appropriate moment to give a list of literary or scientific references to Las Hurdes. The Spanish and French have made frequent contributions in both categories. Nevertheless, we must mention the most precious document of all, the book written in 1927 by the French scholar Maurice Legendre.* For twenty consecutive years he visited the region and conducted a study that is admirable for its depth and scientific rigor.

Professor Legendre says that Las Hurdes resembles no other region in existence, and this on account of two characteristics: misery and pain.

Without any doubt there are many places in the world where people live in precarious and miserable conditions: villages in the Moroccan Atlases, Chinese hamlets, Hindu shantytowns, and so on. But in general, if conditions for the existence of a people become impossible, permanently impossible, that people emigrates en masse in search of sustenance in a less hostile environment. This is not what has happened in Las Hurdes. Individual inhabitants may emigrate, only to return at once. They die

---

*[*Las Jurdes: études de géographie humaine*, Bibliothèque de l'Ecole des hautes études hispaniques 13 (Bordeaux: Feret, 1927).—Trans.]

clinging to their land, and if they are taken from it, they die of longing to return. We found some Hurdanos who spoke French. They had worked in France as day laborers, and as soon as they saved enough money they hurried back. We even found one man who had been to America.

In general, a people in permanent misery either emigrates en masse or their numbers are slowly depleted, until they finally disappear. In Las Hurdes exactly the opposite happens. Instead of decreasing, the number of inhabitants has grown annually, to the point of overpopulation today. How can such an anomaly be explained?

Thus, what distinguishes Las Hurdes as a unique example of human society is not misery but the permanence of that misery, not pain but the perpetuation of that pain.

Predominant in the legend that has formed around Las Hurdes is a belief in its savagery. Nothing could be more contrary to reality. These people could not resemble savage tribes any less. For most tribes, life is paradisiacal. Man has only to reach out his hand to gather the bounty offered to him by nature. No spiritual conflict exists between the savage and reality; a primitive civilization has a correspondingly primitive culture. But in Las Hurdes a primitive civilization corresponds with a contemporary culture. The people share our own moral and religious principles. They speak our language. They have the same needs that we do, but their means of satisfying them are in certain aspects almost neolithic.

I know of no human society that possesses fewer tools than the Hurdanos. Although they are as familiar as we are with the terrible mechanical complexity of our age, the implements they use for work are scarce and rudimentary. In upper Las Hurdes, there are neither plows nor animals for plowing or transport. There are no firearms and no steel weapons. There are hardly any domestic animals; for example, they have neither dogs nor cats. We shall see in the film what kinds of animals do live there. There are no wheeled vehicles of any kind. There are no glasses, bottles, or forks. The list could go on and on.

Imagine my surprise when one day in one of the villages—certainly the best of them—I discovered nothing less than a sewing machine, a bit antiquated and rusty, but a genuine Singer sewing machine.

The few tools that can be seen there have been imported from Castile or Extremadura by Hurdanos who went to beg in those places. Nothing is made in Las Hurdes itself. There is no craft industry. One Hurdano told us he was a baker but hadn't practiced his profession in a very long time since there was no flour to make bread. And this is the main reason for their lack of crafts: the dearth of raw materials due to poverty, which makes it impossible to import them, for the ground in Las Hurdes yields nothing more than heather and rockrose.

And the clothes worn by the Hurdanos? They are like ours: jackets and pants for the men, skirts and blouses for the women. But these have been mended so often that barely a shred of the original material is left. On one piece of clothing I counted seventy-two patches.

Another incredible aspect of this region is that it has no folklore. In all the time we were there, we didn't hear a single song. The people work in complete silence, without the help of song to ease their difficult tasks. The silence of Las Hurdes is unique in the world. In fact, it is not a silence of death; it is a silence of life. Perhaps less poetic than the former, but far more terrible.

Nor did we see drawings on the walls or rocks of Las Hurdes. Nevertheless, at the very entrance to Las Hurdes, in Las Batuecas, can be found one of the most interesting sites of cave art. That is to say, thousands of years ago the region was a focus of human culture, while today those who inhabit these same places no longer know artistic expression.

The Hurdanos are extremely meek by nature. If they speak, it is to lament their misfortune, their slavery in this cruel land. Their customs are simple. Hard daily toil does not leave room for disinterested social interaction. Leisure and pleasant distractions do not exist. Given the small size of their dwellings, all members of a family must live in one room. Such mingling no doubt favors the incest that has been reported in Las Hurdes. This is perhaps the single moral blemish of which they could be accused; but as St. Thomas said, "To be virtuous, one needs a minimum of material well-being." And this requisite is completely lacking in Las Hurdes.

Many solutions have been proposed to resolve this vexing social problem. We are not able to examine these now. We can only say that none of those put into practice has proven effective. Perhaps the best solution was offered to us by an elderly woman of Las Hurdes whom we ran into one day on an improbable path. Upon seeing us, she set down the load of kindling she had been carrying and came toward us. "Are you engineers," she asked us, "and have you come to remedy our poverty? Well, you should know that there is no remedy. If you want to save us from this hell, take us away from here by force, since we won't leave of our own free will."

And indeed, to end the problem of Las Hurdes would require removing its inhabitants by force, sending them to other parts of Spain, and destroying their wretched villages forever.

Legendre supports the elderly woman's thesis when he declares, "Las Hurdes was born of its isolation. Who knows if its drawing near to the world through roads may not end up causing it to disappear." But a highway has now been opened and its inhabitants have yet to escape down it. They're still there, to the bewilderment of sociologists and other thinkers.

If Las Hurdes constitutes a unique example of human society—not only by its expanse and the number of its inhabitants but by other characteristics as well—there are nevertheless other parts of Spain in which life goes on under similar conditions. But these are isolated cases that until now have not drawn the attention of men of science. Moreover, they are about to disappear. Twenty years ago in the Savoy Alps in France there were two villages of this kind. Today only one remains, and it too will probably soon disappear. Just like the villages of Las Hurdes, this village remains on the outer limits of human interaction, and for six months of the year it is completely cut off by snow. Its inhabitants make bread only once a year, and this, along with a few vegetables and some starch, forms the basis of their diet.

Almost all its inhabitants are dwarfs and afflicted with cretinism, and if one of them develops with a normal intelligence, he soon flees the place. That is just one aspect that differentiates this village from Las Hurdes. We have seen that one of the things that is unknown in Las Hurdes is leisure. By contrast, winter imposes a terrible idleness in the Savoy village, confining the inhabitants to their hovels for six months. In those conditions the mix of consanguineous individuals is endemic.

It seems that in Czechoslovakia and Italy as well there also exist villages in which similar conditions are present. But the references I have about these are few, given that there is absolutely no scientific literature on them. I have not visited them. First my professional pursuits and then the state of affairs in Europe during these last few years frustrated plans for a joint expedition with the psychiatrist Dr. Lacan, of l'Hôpital Sainte-Anne in Paris, to these centers of backward civilization that still exist in Europe. But I have not given up hope of someday undertaking it.

I would like to end this introduction with an acknowledgment of the friends who worked selflessly with me to make this film. Our work was done out of love for this miserable region. I, who in the past had found companies and private individuals who made my other films possible, could not obtain enough money to produce this one. Unlike in America, in Europe there are almost no cultural entities or patrons who finance educational films. A humble Spanish worker by the name of Ramón Acín offered me all his resources to make this film. The sum amounted to one thousand dollars. And that was the only capital invested.*

Since we had so little money at our disposal, we had to adapt the technical execution of the film to suit the budget. We had two old cameras loaned by an amateur filmmaker friend in Paris: an old hand-cranked Eclair camera and an ancient Eyemo, from the days when these didn't yet have a drum for attaching different lenses. This latter camera had

---

*[The following six paragraphs, typed single-spaced on a loose sheet, appear to be a later addition to the double-spaced typescript. Although no indication is given, it seems likely they were to be inserted at this point.—Trans.]

one defect. When it began shooting there would be a sharp jump that can still be seen in certain shots.

Film stock was also a problem, since we had almost the precise amount of footage that would later be used to compose the film. So after studying the area for three days, we decided to shoot only those scenes that corresponded to a synopsis written beforehand. Generally, in making a documentary, one films not only those scenes that correspond to a preplanned scenario but also any scenes that arise spontaneously and might later be interesting for the final edit of the film. I was able to do none of that. I divided the script into various segments—for example, food, education, the organization of work, burials, etc.—and each day I set about completing those sequences.

Due to the lack of proper equipment and a complete crew, the work was extremely difficult. During the month and a half we were there, we would get up at four in the morning and arrive at our prearranged location near midday. We would work until three in the afternoon, when we had to start back to where we were staying in Las Batuecas. We made only one meal a day, which we would devour like lions upon returning from work. Physical exertion and a morbid desire to eat in a land where no one eats contributed to that behavior. The first few days, we tried to eat lunch where we were working, but people came from everywhere to see us eat. They watched us avidly, and the children scrambled to pick up salami skins or pieces of bread we had dropped. For that reason we decided not to eat again while working.

All the scenes you see in the film had to be paid for. Our budget was meager, but fortunately it corresponded to the slight claims made by these poor folks. The village of Martinandrán—one of the most miserable—placed itself at our service in exchange for a pair of goats that we had killed and roasted and twenty large loaves of bread, which the town ate collectively during a meal overseen by the mayor, who was perhaps the hungriest of all.

One day we came across a shepherd boy leading several goats, and we asked him if he would mind passing in front of the camera. The boy looked at us, rather frightened. I reached into my pocket and showed him a peseta, a small silver Spanish coin equivalent to a dime. The shepherd eyed it suspiciously. In that same hand I had a few copper coins, and the boy looked at them covetously. As a test, I offered him the equivalent of a penny. The shepherd took it from my hand and agreed at once to be filmed with his goats.

The only lesson that can be drawn from this experience, I think, is that though having a sufficient budget is one of the most important conditions for making a film, it's possible to make the same film if one loves his work.*

Through a strange caprice of that modern Inquisition known as film censoring, a few passages, particularly in the first reel, were suppressed in France, and the result is the film you will see. There are two errors in this first reel that I would now like to correct. These corrections were made in a new version that has been shown in several European countries, but by mistake the version with the uncorrected first reel was sent to me here in America. Apart from a few details of sound, the two errors are these: The text at the beginning of the film says that it was made during the First Spanish Republic. It should read "Second Spanish Republic." The other error is in the title. In Europe the film is known as *Land without Bread*, and not, as you are about to read, *Unpromised Land*.

THE END

*From a typescript in Spanish. N.d.*

---

*[This final paragraph of the addition was handwritten in broken English and has been edited for clarity.—Trans.]

# *Viridiana*

*Viridiana* follows most closely my personal traditions in filmmaking since I made *L'Age d'or* thirty years ago.

Of all my work, these are the two films which I directed with the greatest feeling of freedom.

I have been more or less successful with my films, some of which, to be sure, have been banal. For myself I must say that I made them just to make a living. Equally, however, I must also say that I always refused to make concessions, and I have fought for the principles which were dear to me.

I went back to Spain because that is my country and I could work there with total freedom. I did work there on *Viridiana* with that freedom. What followed was one of those pieces of nonsense that time will take care of.

We do not live in the best of all possible worlds. I would like to continue to make films which, apart from entertaining the audience, convey to people the absolute certainty of this idea. In making such films I believe that my intentions would be highly constructive.

Today movies, including the so-called neorealistic ones, do make it clear that we do not live in the best of all possible worlds.

How is it possible to hope for an improvement in the audiences—and consequently in the producers—when consistently we are told in these films, including even the most insipid comedies, that our social institutions, our concepts of country, religion, love, etc., are, while perhaps imperfect, unique and necessary? The true "opium of the audience" is conformity. The whole film world seems to be dedicated to the propagation of this comfortable feeling, wrapped though it is at times in the insidious disguise of art.

Octavio Paz has said, "But that a man in chains should shut his eyes the world would explode." And I could add, "But that the white eyelid of the screen reflect its proper light the universe would go up in flames." But for the moment we can sleep in peace. The light of the cinema is conveniently dosified and shackled.*

In none of the traditional arts does there exist so wide a gap between the possibilities of what can be done and the facts of what is being done as in the cinema. Motion pictures act directly upon the spectator. To the spectator, persons and things on the screen become concrete.

In the darkness they isolate him from his usual psychic atmosphere. Because of this the cinema is capable of stirring the spectator as perhaps no other art. But as no other art can, it is also capable of stupefying him. The great majority of today's films seem to have exactly that purpose. They thrive in an intellectual and moral vacuum. They imitate the novel. Films repeat over and over the same stories. A fairly educated person would disdainfully throw away any book with the same plot that the greatest films tell us. However, people when sitting in a darkened theater dazzled by light and movement are hypnotized. Apparently even the most cultured person accepts good-humoredly in this environment the silliest topics.

However, for myself, looking across the years I must insist that I have not tried to prove anything and that I do not use the cinema as a pulpit from which I should like to preach. I realize that perhaps I will be disappointing a great many with this statement. But I know that people will draw from *Viridiana* and from my other films many symbols and many meanings.

---

*["Dosified" is Buñuel's English, from the Spanish *dosificar*, to measure out in doses. Compare this paragraph and the next two with the equivalent passage in "Cinema as an Instrument of Poetry," a lecture delivered in Spanish.—Trans.]

I want to make some comments about my film *Viridiana*.

I feel that is very Spanish, and it must be understood that Viridiana was a little-known saint who lived in the period of St. Francis of Assisi.

The story of this picture is born of this situation: A young woman is drugged by an old man; she is at his mercy, whereas in other circumstances he could never be able to hold her in his arms.

I thought that this woman had to be pure, and so I made her a novice preparing to take her final vows.

The idea of the beggars came later, because I thought it would be a natural thing that beggars should be cared for by a nun on her estate. Then I thought to myself that I should like to see these beggars in this estate's dining room at a table covered by an embroidered tablecloth and candles.

All of a sudden the idea took shape in my mind that they should take positions in a sort of tableau, and Leonardo da Vinci's painting came into my mind.

Finally, I associated the "Hallelujah" of Handel's *Messiah* with the dance of the beggars. To me it was more striking than the rhythms of rock and roll; also, I felt within myself that it was particularly fitting to have the Mozart *Requiem* for the love scene between the old man and the young woman and to contrast the sweet sounds of the Angelus with the sound of the labor of the workmen.

I know I have been criticized for having shown a knife in the shape of a crucifix. One finds them everywhere in Spain, and I saw many of them in Albacete. I didn't invent them. It is the photography which stresses the malice and the surrealistic character of an object fabricated innocently and put into mass production.

I am also reproached for my cruelty. In the film—where is it?—the novice proves her humanity. The old man, a complicated human being, is capable of kindness toward human beings and toward a lowly bee whose life he does not hesitate to rescue. His son is rather a sympathetic character. The beggars, of a classic type in Spain, can express their crudeness without cruelty. Only the blind man is distrustful, as are those who have his affliction. For this reason my blind people have moments of nastiness.

In reality, *Viridiana* is a picture of *l'humour noir*, without doubt corrosive, but unplanned and spontaneous, in which I express certain erotic and religious obsessions of my childhood.

I belong to a very Catholic family, and from the age of eight to fifteen I was brought up by Jesuits. However, for me religious education and surrealism have left their marks all through my life.

Concerning *Viridiana*, once again: I think that it has in it most of the themes which are closest to me and which are my most cherished interests.

*From a typescript in English. N.d.*

# To PECIME

(Asociación de periodistas cinematográficos
y de espectáculos de México)

Before we begin the screening of *Viridiana*, and by courtesy of PECIME president Fernando Morales Ortiz, I extend a warm greeting to my friends from PECIME and gladly offer the words that have been asked of me.

*Viridiana*, at heart, is a humorous film; its humor is doubtless corrosive, but spontaneous and unpremeditated. Contrary to what has been said, I did not set out to prove anything through its images; I do not expound a thesis, send messages, or ever use the cinema as a lectern or pulpit. *Viridiana* follows the same personal tradition that began when I made *L'Age d'or* thirty-two years ago in Paris. In both films I express certain obsessions from childhood and adolescence, without having planned it so. I come from a very Catholic family, and from the age of seven to fifteen I was educated by the Jesuits. My religious education and subsequent surrealist experience left indelible marks on my way of seeing and feeling.*

In *Viridiana* there is no deliberate intention to blaspheme or be profane. If some sanctimonious sort thinks he discerns an impious image, it is because that's how it presented itself to my spirit. Had other, more pious, ones come up, perhaps I would have made room for them too. In

---

*[Buñuel's essay on *Viridiana*, in English, presents some of the same material as this lecture in Spanish (although there he dates his Jesuit education to age eight).— Trans.]

principle, I accepted all those scenes or details that moved me, without submitting them to any customary moral dictate or to the criticism of any religious creed whatsoever.

My reason for having gone to Spain to shoot the film was very simple: I love the land of my birth. What's more, I was able to work on the film with complete freedom. I am sorry to disappoint those who believe that miserably concealed behind symbols is an attack on a particular political regime. Nothing was further from my mind. The roots of *Viridiana* were fed by my own nonconformism, which recognizes neither borders nor regimes. There isn't a single consciously introduced symbol in this film. I wrote the plot in Mexico with Julio Alejandro, since at first the idea was to make the film here. But coming into contact again with the Spanish soil I had left twenty-five years earlier was bound to give new form and direction to my ideas, assailed as they were by a multitude of images and intimate memories. That undoubtedly is the source of the profoundly Spanish character that many seem to find in *Viridiana*.

I would like to take this opportunity to pay homage to Silvia Pinal, who so marvelously portrayed the main character.* Modesty, self-effacement, and simplicity are, to my mind, the main qualities of her performance. Only the greatest and very rarest of actors achieve such a total effacement of their real personality for the sake of a fictional one.

*From a typescript in Spanish. N.d.*

---

*[Born in 1931 in Guaymas, Mexico, Silvia Pinal would also star in *The Exterminating Angel* and *Simon of the Desert*.—Trans.]

# AUTOBIOGRAPHICAL WRITINGS

# Fragments of a Journal from Buñuel's Youth in Calanda

*December 28, 1913*

After breakfast I went to look for Pepe, who was already better, and the two of us together went to look for Joaquín. Then we went to play billiards, and later, with Emilio, to my place to play cards. The bell struck for the eleven o'clock mass, so off we went. When it ended, it was back to Joaquín's house, where Carmen and the three of us played cards. After that I went to eat at my Uncle Santos's house. Since it was Holy Innocents' Day, I bought, as a joke on Aurelia and Carmen, euphorbia powders, which can make anyone sneeze, but seeing as they were both on their guard, the only innocent one was me, since, having tried the powders to see if it was true that they made you sneeze, I couldn't stop for two hours. . . .

*December 29, 1913*

When I got dressed this morning I put on my leggings, the belt with eleven cartridges, and my straw hat, since we were going to La Fuensalada to see the pigs killed and, at the same time, to see if we could shoot a few thrushes, but all we could flush out were some herons and crows that flew off before they saw us. Meanwhile, thousands of birds flew up that I didn't want to shoot, but since I was sick of not having fired a single shot, I turned to shoot at a bullfinch, but the intense cold, the snow, and the fierce wind had so swollen my fingers that I couldn't pull the trigger. We had something to eat there and . . .

*January 2, 1914*

At nine thirty I went to look for Joaquín. While the other two played, we read *Marcof.* . . . After lunch I went back to Joaquín's, where we amused ourselves with a pig bladder hung from the ceiling as a punching bag. . . .

*January 3, 1914*

At lunch I went to look for Joaquín and Pepito, and the three of us played cards in the dining room. After eating, we went to Don Luis's house to work on the parallel bars and to fence. . . . Then we went home to prepare glass negatives to make photographs. After dinner we talked for a while, then went to bed. It was a splendid day.

*From the Spanish. Written in 1913–14 (Buñuel was thirteen years old).*

# Medieval Memories
of Lower Aragón

I was barely fourteen when I left Aragón for the first time. I was invited to the home of some friends, a family that summered in Vega de Pas (Santander). While crossing the Basque country I marveled at its landscape, the polar opposite of the landscape of what up to then had been my "habitat." Fog, rain, a humid forest full of moss and ferns . . . It was a delicious impression that still persists in my memory. I love the north, the cold, the snow, the great mountains cut through by raging rivers.

My homeland in Lower Aragón is fertile but austere and extremely dry. A year could go by, maybe even two, without a cloud crossing its impassive sky. Drought was a permanent worry. When a cumulus appeared behind the mountains several laborers and members of the Industrial and Mercantile Club would come to my house—which was crowned with a small turretlike observatory—to track its slow advance and sadly announce, "Southern wind. It'll pass us by." And sure enough, the cloud would float away without shedding a drop of water on the fields.

In my village—at the time of my early teens, around 1913—one might say that we lived in the Middle Ages. It was an isolated, unchanging society, with a very marked class difference. The respect and subordination of the working class toward the landed gentry was absolute. Life in the town, as directed by the bells in the tower of Our Lady of Pilar, glided by horizontally in an admirable and ordered stillness, especially if we compare it with the horrible maelstrom and hurried pace of our lives today. The bells rang out the religious hours: masses, vespers, the Angelus, the death knell. The sounds of the great bell, grave and profound, signaled the death of an adult, while bells of a lighter metal, with a less sad tone, announced the death of a child. The bells rang furiously for a fire or swung gloriously for Sundays and feast days. Fewer than five thousand people lived in my village, Calanda.

The village was eleven miles from Alcañiz, which could be reached by train from Zaragoza. Few strangers came to Calanda, except during the festivities for the Virgin of Pilar or the September fair. But every day around noon, Macán's stagecoach would appear in a cloud of dust, drawn by mules. It brought the mail and the odd business traveler. The first car in town was a Ford bought by Don Luis González in 1919. He was modern and liberal, a perfect example of nineteenth-century anticlericalism. His mother, Doña Trinidad, was a refined woman from a noble Sevillian family, the widow of a general who had served as adjutant to Espartero. But the ladies in town avoided her company, thanks to certain indiscretions by her domestics. That contraption Doña Trinidad used for washing her intimate parts scandalized the chaste ladies who, with big gestures, indignantly drew the outline of an object resembling a guitar.

This same Don Luis played an important role when the phylloxera infestation struck Lower Aragón. The vineyards were dying with no solution in sight. The farmers flatly refused to uproot their grapevines and replace them with American ones. An agricultural engineer came from Teruel to set up a microscope in city hall showing a sample vine, so that the villagers could see with their own eyes how it was crawling with lice. But still they refused to replace the diseased plants with ones resistant to the pest. Don Luis pulled out all his grapevines and, since he received death threats, carried his rifle as he walked through his vineyard newly planted with American grapes. The collective stubbornness so typical of Aragón yielded before the evidence, and soon the change was accepted.

Lower Aragón produces the finest oil in all of Spain. In some years the harvest was splendid, but in years of drought, parasites would leave

the trees bare of fruit. The farmers of Calanda, considered great special-
ists, were sought out to prune olive trees in Jaen and Córdoba. The har-
vest started at the beginning of winter, and the workers used to sing the
*Jota olivarera* in two-part harmony. While the men, up on ladders, used
sticks to hit the branches loaded with fruit, the women would collect the
olives from the ground. The *Jota olivarera* is sweet, melodious, and deli-
cate—at least, that is how I remember it—in curious contrast with the
brazen force of the regional songs of Aragón.

Another song from that time that is forever engraved in my memory,
floating between wakefulness and sleep—one I think has been lost to-
day, because the melody was transmitted orally from generation to gen-
eration without ever being transcribed—was "the song of aurora." Be-
fore dawn, a group of youngsters would run through the streets waking
up the harvesters, who had to start their work at daybreak. Surely some
of those "wake-up singers" must still be alive and could pass on the
words and melody to a composer so that the song does not disap-
pear forever. That indescribable chorus, partly religious, partly profane,
of an already bygone era would wake me up in the middle of the night.
Conversely, all year long a pair of night watchmen, equipped with
lanterns and nightsticks, would guard our sleep. "Praise the Lord,"
shouted one, and the other responded, "May He always be praised,"
"Eleven o'clock," "Calm skies," or rarely—what joy!—"cloudy" or, un-
expectedly, "raining."

Every Friday morning a group of elderly men and women—the
town's poor folk—would sit next to the walls of the church, across from
my house. One of our servants would give each of them a piece of bread,
which they kissed respectfully, and a ten-cent coin, a generous sum
compared to the "penny-apiece" meted out by the other rich families
in town.

Apparently the famous drums of Holy Week date back to the end of
the eighteenth century, and the tradition died out at the beginning of
this century. Mosen Vicente Allanegui revived it. Now they play drums
almost without pause from noon on Good Friday to the same time on

Saturday. Their noise evokes the darkness and the crashing of rocks that shook the world at the moment of Christ's death. And in effect, their sonic conjuring makes the earth shake and the walls shudder; the ground vibrations move through your feet up to your chest. If you put your hand on a wall, you can confirm this incredible phenomenon. In my time, there were hardly two hundred drummers beating the skins. Today there are over a thousand drums.

I also recall my earliest encounters with death, which, together with a profound religious faith and the awakening of my sexual instinct, frame my experiences as an adolescent. One day I was walking with my father through an olive grove when a sweet and repugnant odor drifted over to us on the breeze. Some hundred yards away, a dozen vultures were feasting on a dead donkey that was horribly bloated. The spectacle simultaneously attracted and repelled me. The birds so gorged themselves that they could hardly fly. Farmers did not bury dead animals, believing that the decomposing carcasses would fertilize their soil. I was fascinated by this vision, and apart from its gross materiality, I had a vague intuition of its metaphysical significance. My father took me by the arm and led me away.

On another occasion one of the shepherds that cared for our flock was fatally stabbed in the back during a foolish argument. Young men used to keep a good knife on their belts. The autopsy was performed in the cemetery chapel by the town doctor, with the barber as his assistant. Four or five other people, friends of the doctor, were present as spectators, and I managed to mix in with them. There were many rounds of brandy, and I drank anxiously to keep up my courage, which began to waver as I heard the saw open the cranium or the dull crack of a breaking rib. I ended up monumentally drunk. They had to carry me home, where my father punished me for getting drunk and being a "sadist."

And the funerals of the poor, with their coffins in the plaza before the open door of the church. The priests would recite the prayer for the dead, and the parish priest would walk around the coffin sprinkling it with holy water from his aspergillum. Then, half opening the coffin, he would throw a shovelful of ashes on the chest of the corpse. The bell with the deep ring would continue to sound, and as the coffin was carried to the graveyard, the mother of the deceased would scream uncontrollably: "Oh, my beloved son! You have left me all alone. I'll never see you again."

Death was ever present, as in the Middle Ages.

By contrast, the joy of living was much stronger. The pleasures, always desired, were far more intense. The greater the obstacles between desire and its realization, the more intense the enjoyment when they are overcome. The same thing happens with love. Ease turns powerful emotion into banality. Beauty must be conquered. In Zaragoza the schedule of concerts that the philharmonic society was preparing for the winter was passed out in October. You had to wait for months to hear, for example, the Fifth Symphony. How impatiently we awaited that moment, which, when it finally arrived, gave us an indescribable satisfaction, a nearly divine happiness. Today you just have to push the button of a radio or a record player and you have music. But there is no doubt that the pleasure is not the same, no matter how good the hi-fi or stereo system is. Saturation diminishes pleasure.

Notwithstanding the sincerity and the vividness of our faith, we could not keep constant sexual impulses in check. At twelve I still believed that babies came from Paris, until a somewhat older friend initiated me into that great mystery. From that moment on, sex took on its tyrannical function. The most commendable virtue, we had been taught, was chastity, which now clashed with my instincts, generating a terrible conflict and feelings of guilt at violating, if only in thought, that virtue. In summer, during the siesta, in the torrid heat and with the incessant buzzing of flies in the empty streets, I used to get together with a group of boys my age in the shade of a clothing store, with its doors locked and curtains drawn. There the clerk would show us "erotic" magazines—God only knows where he found them: *The Figleaf* and *K.D.T,* the latter having more realistic illustrations than the clumsy drawings of *The Figleaf.* Those forbidden magazines would seem pristinely innocent today. The most you could see was a hint of a thigh or a breast, but that was enough to inflame our desire or incite our secrets. The complete separation of men and women made our impulses all the more urgent.

Don Leoncio, one of the town doctors, would have laughed at our moral conflict had he known. He was a strong spirit, anticlerical and staunchly republican. The walls of his office were covered from top to bottom with the colored covers of *REVOLT*, a fiercely anticlerical anarchist magazine that was very popular in Spain at that time. I remember one of those covers. Two big, fat priests were driving a carriage drawn by Christ, who was sweating and grimacing with pain. To give a sense of what that magazine was about, here is how they described a workers' rally in Madrid, with its consequent violence and injuries: "Yesterday afternoon a group of workers was walking peacefully up Montera Street toward San Luis Circle when they saw two priests coming down the street on the opposite sidewalk. Given such provocation . . ." etc.

But our faith remained intact. Never would we have doubted the miracle of Miguel Pellicer, visited in his sleep one night by the Virgin of Pilar, who, with the help of two angels, restored his leg that had been amputated a year ago, a leg that was "dead and buried." My father gave the Church of Our Lady of Pilar in Calanda a processional float with life-size figures portraying the miracle. It was destroyed during the Civil War.

My family only spent summers in Calanda. Upon returning from Cuba, where he had amassed a small fortune, my father had a house built that so impressed the simple folk that even people from nearby villages would come to see it. It was furnished and decorated in the taste of the time—the "bad taste" of the time, which eventually was vindicated by the history of art. The greatest representative of this style in Spain was Gaudí, who today is considered an architectural genius.

Whenever the great door of the house was open to let someone in, you could always see several girls, about eight to ten years old, standing or sitting just outside and gaping at what for them was a most "luxurious" interior. Almost all of them held in their arms a very young brother, too small to shoo the flies that would land now on his eyelids, now on the corner of his lips. The mothers of these little nannies were out working the fields or bustling about at home before preparing potatoes and beans for dinner, the permanent staple of the working-class diet.

Outside the village, on the banks of the Guadalope River, we had a country house with a luxuriant, well-landscaped garden, where the whole family would go every afternoon in two carts, each pulled by a horse. Our cartload of merry kids would often pass by a barefooted lad picking horse droppings off the road and putting them in a miserable basket for his father to use in fertilizing his small garden plot. This humble and heartbreaking vision left us completely indifferent. On many nights we would dine in the yard, with an abundant and delicious spread of food illuminated by carbide lamps. The leisurely life, sweet and splendid. If instead of being one of the *señores* I had been among those who worked the land by the sweat of their brow, perhaps my memories would be less pleasing.

Without a doubt we were at the end of an ancient way of life. Commercial trade was limited, and the production of oil was the only industry in the village. Fabrics and hardware supplies came from outside, as did medicine, or rather its ingredients, which the pharmacist would mix according to the doctor's prescription.

Local craftsmen provided all the necessities of the neighborhood: leather workers, tinsmiths, blacksmiths, bakers, masons, weavers at their loom and shuttle, potters making primitive jugs and bowls, etc. The agricultural economy of the region was semifeudal. Landowners let sharecroppers cultivate their land in exchange for half the harvest.

In Calanda there are no longer any poor people going out on Fridays to beg for bread. Today it's a relatively rich town, and its people are well dressed. The traditional attire of pants, satchel, and neckerchief has disappeared. There are sewers, running water, paved streets, movie theaters, bars, and television galore, which, here as everywhere else in the world, does its part to turn viewers into dullards and extroverts. There are cars, motorcycles, and refrigerators. There is the material happiness brought by our "marvelous" consumer society, whose scientific and technological advances have taken priority over the development of the most cherished values—moral and spiritual—of mankind. Entropy or chaos is already heralded by the distressing syndrome of population explosion.

I had the good fortune of spending my childhood in the Middle Ages, that "painful and exquisite" time as described by the French author Huysmans: painful in terms of material life, but spiritually exquisite. Precisely the opposite of today.

*From the Spanish. Published in* El Libro de Aragón CAZAR, 1876–1976 *(Madrid: ASTYGI, 1976)*.

# From Buñuel's Autobiography

I was born on February 22, 1900, in Calanda, a town in the province of Teruel, Spain.

My father had spent almost all his life in America, where, as a wholesale merchant, he succeeded in amassing something of a fortune. When well in his forties he decided to return to his native town, Calanda, where he married my mother, who was then barely seventeen. I was the first of the seven children of this marriage who are now living in Spain.

My infancy slipped by in an almost medieval atmosphere (like that of nearly all Spanish provinces) between my native town and Zaragoza. I feel it necessary to say here (since it explains in part the trend of the modest work which I later accomplished) that the two basic sentiments of my childhood, which stayed with me well into adolescence, are those of profound eroticism, at first sublimated in a great religious faith, and a permanent consciousness of death. It would take too long here to analyze the reasons. Suffice it to say that I was not an exception among my compatriots, since this is a very Spanish characteristic, and our art, an exponent of the Spanish spirit, was impregnated with these two sentiments. The last civil war, peculiar and ferocious as no other, exposed them clearly.

My eight years as a student with the Jesuit fathers only increased these sentiments instead of diminishing them. Until my baccalaureate at sixteen years of age, one can say that I had not been a part of modern society.* I went to Madrid to study. The change from the province to the capital was as amazing to me as it would have been to a crusader who suddenly found himself on Fifth Avenue, New York City.

When I graduated with my bachelor degree my father asked me what I wanted to study. I had two chief interests: one, music (I had taken several violin courses), and the other, natural sciences. I asked my father to allow me to go to Paris and enroll in the Schola Cantorum and continue the study of composition. He refused, arguing that with the career of an artist one was more apt to die of hunger than to prosper. This was the attitude of any Spanish father (and perhaps of a father of any nationality). Flattering my other interest, he urged me to go to Madrid to study for the career of Agricultural Engineer.

In 1917 I therefore found myself settled in Madrid in the Students' Residence, which in Spain is the only really modern institution of pedagogy, inspired and created, in imitation of the English universities, by the Institución Libre de Enseñanza.

A curious thing is that in Spain the careers of engineers are the most difficult and honorable which a young man can pursue.† The aristocratic thing to do in Spain is to study to be an engineer or a diplomat. The only young men who had access to these careers were those who, beside having the necessary intelligence and application, had sufficient funds, as the cost was excessive for the modest Spanish way of living.

In agricultural engineering there was the absurd situation in which, although it was essentially a career of natural sciences, it was necessary for one to study mathematics for several years. And if my inclinations led me to the study of nature, I in no way felt inclined to solve equations with the grade of $n$. Nevertheless, I studied mathematics for three years. With this they succeeded in making me hate my studies.

*[Buñuel uses "baccalaureate" and "bachelor degree" in the sense of the Spanish *bachillerato*, or completion of high school.—Trans.]

†[Buñuel uses "career" as a cognate of Spanish *carrera*, a course of study or major.—Trans.]

Determined to try on my own and without my father's permission, I enrolled in 1920 as a pupil of the learned Spanish entomologist, Dr. Bolivar, director of the Museum of Natural History of Madrid. This and the following year I dedicated to the study of insects, which, as far as my material future was concerned, was less lucrative than if I had studied music at the Schola Cantorum.

I worked with interest for over a year, although I soon arrived at the conclusion that I was more interested in the life or literature of insects than in their anatomy, physiology, and classification.

During that time I formed a close friendship, at the Students' Residence, with a group of young artists who were to influence me strongly in finding my bent. Some of them have become famous, such as the poet Federico García Lorca, the painter Salvador Dalí, Moreno Villa, poet and critic, etc. I began to collaborate in the vanguard of literary publications, publishing some poems and preferring to chat with my friends in the cafe rather than to sit at the table with the microscope at the Museum of Natural History.

My new literary leanings made me realize that my goal was arts and letters rather than natural sciences. Thus I changed my career and began the study of Philosophy and Letters in the University of Madrid, and graduated with a degree in 1924.

I cannot say that I was a good student. I alternated between interminable gatherings of our group of friends and the writing of poems and sports. In 1921 I became amateur boxing champion of Spain, because, as the saying goes, "In the land of the blind the one-eyed man is king."

Upon completing my career, I found myself at loose ends. My only out was to try for a professorship in an institute or university, a profession for which I felt I had no calling. I was twenty-four years old and realized that I must think seriously about getting established, but nevertheless I felt more undecided and perplexed than ever. This is a fault prevailing among the Spanish. Instead of a youth's developing according to his likes and aptitudes, he must follow the course marked out by his parents. The student, upon leaving the bosom of his family and feeling himself independent, is more drawn to life itself than to study. The Spanish University did very little, one must realize, to attract the students or inspire their affection.

My nervousness and uncertainty were dissipated immediately when my mother gave me permission to go to Paris. My father had died the year before.

In 1925 I arrived in Paris without having any idea of what was to become of me. I wanted to do something—work, earn my living—but I didn't know how. I continued writing poems, but this seemed to me more like the luxury of a *señorito*. Then, as even now, I was opposed to luxury and to the *señoritos*, although by birth I was one of them.

Among the Spaniard's many defects is that of improvisation, which arises from the belief that he knows everything. I must confess that this fault was a virtue for me, since thanks to it I found my walk of life, and in a profession which appears to be conclusive for me. Because I could improvise I was able to make my debut as *metteur en scène* in Amsterdam, directing the scenic part of *El Retablo de Maese Pedro*.

I had gone to Paris with a letter of introduction to the illustrious pianist Ricardo Viñes. One day when I was calling on him, Viñes told me that the director of the Dutch orchestra, Maestro Mengelberg, had told him to gather all kinds of artistic elements in Paris, in order to present in Amsterdam *El Retablo de Maese Pedro*, a musical composition for orchestra, voice, and stage by Manuel de Falla.

The aforementioned work, perhaps the most exquisite of the Spanish master, had up to then been given only once, in the palace of Princess de Polignac, in Paris. The princess had expressly commissioned Falla to do it.

*El Retablo de Maese Pedro* is an episode taken from *Don Quixote de la Mancha*. In the play are Don Quixote, Sancho, and other Cervantes characters who are present during the performance of a puppet show put on by Maese Pedro. At the performance in the home of Princess de Polignac both the Cervantes characters, as well as the puppets, had been dolls.

It occurred to me to "improvise": I suggested to Viñes that the human characters be actors, altering their faces with masks, so that in this way there might be a more pronounced difference between them and the puppets, which could only be dolls. It seemed a good idea to him and I offered to execute it. I still can't understand why he accepted. I was named *régisseur* and consequently charged with the scenic part.

I looked among my friends for the eight flesh-and-blood characters which we needed. Or to be more accurate, I added their inexperience to mine, inasmuch as one was a painter, another a medical student, still another a newspaperman, and none actors.

The decorations, costumes, masks, and dolls were commissioned from good artists in Paris. The singers were from the Opera Comica, among others Vera Yanocopulos, and they were to sing from the orchestra. The characters in the play had to follow the action of the song with pantomime.

I still tremble when I think of my audacity and that of my friends, who accepted in order to be able to visit Amsterdam gratis. Collaborating with Falla, one the greatest contemporary musicians; with Mengelberg, a famous orchestra conductor; with singers of the Opera Comica. Orchestra seats for the premiere sold at 200 francs. This spectacle formed the most discordant and heterogeneous conglomeration which music and the theater have ever seen together.

I must say that we didn't do so badly, and that both my friends and I gave all our efforts to succeed in such a disproportionate enterprise. None of the public suspected that the plastic part of the spectacle was an experiment, for once not catastrophic, of Spanish improvisation. I should add that we had been having rehearsals for a month.

Drunk with my success, which it was for me by virtue of not being a failure, I felt that a great love of the *mise en scène* had awakened within me. Shortly afterward, in Paris, I saw a film by Fritz Lang, *Les Trois Lu-*

*mières,*\* which greatly impressed me. For the first time I felt that the movies could be a vehicle of expression and not merely a pastime, which up to then I had thought them. I succeeded in getting Jean Epstein, who was then the most famous director in France, to take me as an assistant. I worked with him for two years and with him learned the technical side of moving pictures.

In 1929 I entered the surrealist group of Paris. Its moral and artistic intransigence, its new social political field fit in perfectly with my temperament. As I was the only moving picture person in the group, I decided to take the aesthetics of surrealism to the screen.

That same year I asked my mother for $2,500 to make my first cinematographic experiment. Only she would have financed an idea that seemed ridiculous to everyone else. My mother gave me the money more out of love than understanding of my venture, which I was careful not to explain to her.

Thus I produced my first film, which was at the same time the first surrealist film, entitled *Un Chien andalou.* It is a two-reel short in which there are neither dogs nor Andalusians. The title had the virtue of becoming an obsession with some people, among others the American writer Harry V. Miller, who, without knowing me, wrote me an extraordinary letter, which I still have, about his obsession.

In the film are amalgamated the aesthetics of surrealism with Freudian discoveries. It answered the general principle of that school, which defines surrealism as "an unconscious, psychic automatism, able to return to the mind its real function, outside of all control exercised by reason, morality, or aesthetics."

Although I availed myself of oneiric elements the film is not the description of a dream. On the contrary, the environment and characters are of a realistic type. Its fundamental difference from other films consists in the fact that the characters function animated by impulses, the primal sources of which are confused with those of irrationalism, which,

\*[The French title for *Der müde Tod* (1921); cf. pp. 99 and 258.—Trans.]

in turn, are those of poetry. At times these characters react enigmatically, inasfar as a pathologic psychic complex can be enigmatic.

The film is directed at the unconscious feelings of man, and therefore is of universal value, although it may seem disagreeable to certain groups of society which are sustained by puritanical moral principles.

When I made the film I was absolutely sure that it was going to be a failure, but I didn't care because I had the conviction that it expressed something until then never said in pictures. Above all it was sincere.

The film was christened in June 1929, in the Ursulines theater in Paris, before a select public. I was stupefied, confused, by the avalanche of enthusiasm which its showing awakened. I actually believed it was a joke. It was not, since it ran for nine consecutive months in the moving picture theater Studio 28, for the general public. Hundreds of articles were written and controversies were started. Other films were made along the same line, such as *La Perle* by Georges Hugnet and *Bateaux parisiens* by Gorel, and other attempts which were not very successful.

Shortly after the opening of *Un Chien andalou*, Georges-Henri Rivière, assistant director of the Trocadéro museum and an intimate friend of Vicomte de Noailles, patrons and exquisite generous people, called me. Rivière took me to their home and introduced me. My present friends, Charles and Marie-Laure de Noailles, wanted to give me the means to make another film, in which they gave me complete liberty in the choice of subject. They only asked that the score of the film be written by Stravinsky. I had to refuse the latter, since my surrealist discipline and the artistic tendencies of our group were incompatible with those of Stravinsky, above all from a moral standpoint. The patrons agreed to do without the musician, and the score was taken from fragments of classical music. So my second film was called *L'Age d'or*.

It consists of six reels. It was one of the first talkies made in France and cost about $25,000, a small amount if one considers the ambitiousness of the film.

The story is also a sequence of moral and surrealist aesthetic. Around two principal characters, a man and woman, is disclosed the existing conflict in all human society between the sentiment of love and any other sentiment, of a religious, patriotic, humanitarian order; here also the setting and characters are realistic, but the hero is animated by egoism which imagines all attitudes amorous, to the exclusion of control or other sentiments. *The sexual instinct and the sense of death* form the substance of the film, a romantic film performed in full surrealistic frenzy. In it were certain experiments in the use of sound and speech which were later used in commercial films. For example, in *A nous la liberté* by René Clair, a love scene in a garden. Jean Cocteau produced, a year later, *Le Sang d'un poète*,* also subsidized by the Noailles, in which film the great influence of *L'Age d'or* can be noticed.

When this film was first shown the whole surrealistic group launched a manifesto on the purpose of *L'Age d'or*, which was answered by Léon Daudet, from *L'Action française*, an extreme rightist paper, inciting their initiates to attack the theater. The attack by reactionary young Frenchmen was brought to an end six days after the first showing of the film, causing damages in the theater and vestibule to the amount of 120,000 francs. The projection continued two days more in the devastated place, and as the partisans of the film wanted to exercise reprisals, the chief of police in Paris, Chiappe, suspended the showing. Deputy Gaston Bergery appealed to the Congress in behalf of the film, although to no avail.

Hundred of articles were written about the film, some for, others against; and whenever it was shown, either in France or outside, it was at private societies or theaters. Its producers, the Vicomte and Vicomtesse de Noailles, withdrew it from circulation in 1934 to keep it in their archives, since it was almost impossible to actually show it.

After making *L'Age d'or* I received some offers to make films of a commercial type which I had to refuse, not because they were commercial but because I disagreed with the theme.

In 1932 I separated from the surrealist group, although I remained on good terms with my ex-companions. I was beginning not to agree with

*[Buñuel calls the film *La Vie d'un poète*.—Trans.]

that kind of intellectual aristocracy, with its artistic and moral extremes, which isolated us from the world and limited us to our own company. Surrealists considered the majority of mankind contemptible or stupid, and thus withdrew from all social participation and responsibility and shunned the work of the others.

To earn a living I began to collaborate anonymously in my profession, entering as a writer in Paramount Studios in Paris, adapting pictures from English to Spanish. I was then supervisor for "dubbing" at Warner Bros. in Madrid. I have a pleasant memory of my association with that company and of its chief in Spain, Mr. Huet.

If I left Warner Bros. it was only because I began to produce pictures in Spain for my country and for South America. For this purpose I entered partnership with a young Spanish financier, Mr. Urgoiti, who owned the best chain of theaters in Madrid. I was the anonymous producer of several films made by Filmofono, which was the name of the company. Although it had started, there did not yet exist in Spain the specialized work of the Hollywood studios, and I had to develop directors, writers, etc. The pictures were an economic success, the principal ones being *Don Quintín el amargao, La Hija de Juan Simón, ¿Quién me quiere a mi?, ¡Centinela, alerta!* They are nevertheless mediocre if compared from an artistic standpoint to similar American ones, although intellectually and morally they are no worse than those which the Hollywood studios produce.

Our experiment was going marvelously, when the work was suddenly stopped by the Spanish Civil War on July 18, 1936.

Between 1932 and 1936 I made only one picture under my own name. It was shown in Paris in 1937, although its completion dated from 1933. This picture was called *Land without Bread*.

There exists in Spain a section almost unknown by the Spanish, until King Alfonso made a trip to it in 1925. It still remains on the outskirts of Spanish life and civilization, its obstinacy a social problem and enigma.

This section, called Las Hurdes, is one of the most miserable on the face of the globe, isolated from the outside world by mountains difficult to pass and with a population of six thousand inhabitants distributed in fifty-two hamlets.

It originated at the beginning of the sixteenth century, when some of the survivors of the Jewish expulsion and persecution ordered by the Catholic kings went to inhabit it. Its population was increased later by outlaws who were seeking refuge in this mountains, fleeing the rigors of justice.

Only sixty miles from Salamanca, one of the centers of European culture, and two miles from Las Batuecas, one of the most interesting centers of Paleolithic culture, Las Hurdes nevertheless has remained unbelievably backward.

Bread is almost unknown in Las Hurdes Altas. The inhabitants have to work, with great effort, their fields which barely yield enough to sustain them for nine months. They almost completely lack utensils or work implements. There are no domestic animals. There is no folklore. During the two months I stayed there I didn't hear one song, nor see a single picture, in their little shacks and hovels. Impoverishment, hunger, and incest, a product of the horrible misery, have made many inhabitants cretinous. Nevertheless, the majority possess normal mental faculties, being rather quick in intelligence.

The pathetic thing about this country, and for this reason its psychological and human interest is very superior to that of barbaric tribes, is that though its material civilization is rudimentary and almost prehistoric, its religious and moral culture and ideas are like those of any civilized country. There are Hurdanos who speak French because they have emigrated. Why don't these people entirely abandon their country? Geographers are agreed that it is uninhabitable. Neither books nor the film have been able to explain the reason for their continuance there.

Through the trips of the king and the magnificent book of the French professor Mr. Legendre on this country which he studied profoundly for twenty years, I became acquainted with its existence, and my desire was to make an objective document, a sort of human geographical study about it. However, no one wanted to give me the little money I asked for in order to produce it. Some it repelled, others were afraid of losing their money, the rest said that it wasn't fair to show Spain in that light. As if hiding the truth would remedy the evil.

A laborer from Huesca, Ramón Acín, to whom I had spoken of this project in friendly conversation, became very much interested by my idea and offered me part of his savings for the undertaking. He could only give me $2,000.* Considering the smallness of the budget, I looked in Paris for disinterested collaborators and friends whom I succeeded in making love Las Hurdes. The poet Pierre Unik, the cameraman Eli Lotar, professor Sánchez Ventura and the producer Ramón Acín helped me in my enterprise. We passed two months that were unforgettable for all of us in that remote civilization.

There are French and English versions of the film, and it had a very good reception by the public in France and Belgium. It was also shown in England and Holland. Now I am bringing it to North America.

When the civil war broke out, I stopped all cinematographic work and placed myself at the disposal of the government, which sent me to Paris as attaché to the Spanish Embassy in that capital. In 1938, about eight months ago, I arrived in the U.S.A. on a diplomatic mission, and here I was surprised by the end of the war. As I could legally remain in the United States, I plan to stay here indefinitely, intensely attracted by the American naturalness and sociability.

### My Present Plans

I have already said that my cinematographic activities were completely interrupted by the Spanish conflict, and it has been exactly three years since I have practiced my profession. Because of both a spiritual as well as material urge, I must return to work, the latter reason emphasized by the fact that I am married and have a son.

*[In his Spanish essay on *Land without Bread*, Buñuel recalls the sum as $1,000.— Trans.]

One of the avenues suggested to me is to look for a position in Hollywood cinematography, something if not impossible, at least difficult in view of present conditions in the industry.

Another field is independent production. And I call it independent in the artistic sense, as the so-called independent productions here are perhaps more dependent than the others on commercial routine and demands. Well and good: this type of independent film to which I refer has disappeared almost completely because of the great cost of production.

I believe that the most interesting experiments which are made today are to be found in documentary films, which are in reality the successors to the aforementioned "independent productions."

To my mind, there exist two different types of documentary films: one which can be called *descriptive*, and in which the material is limited to the transcription of a natural or social phenomenon. For example: industrial manufacture, the construction of a road, or the operations of some aviation line, etc. etc. Another type, much less frequent, is one which, while both descriptive and objective, tries to interpret reality. It can, for this reason, appeal to the artistic emotions of the spectator and express love, sorrow, and humor. Such a documentary film is much more complete, because besides illustrating, it is moving.

Although there are themes which lend themselves more readily than others to such a purpose, none are excluded a priori from this emotional possibility. The banal action of building a road or showing a new aviation line, to which we referred before, can, according to its interpretation, become dramatic, comic, or subversive.

Documentary films generally bore a public not versed in that subject. More material than necessary is used to bring out details whose value is solely visual or dynamic. The great majority of documentary films lack psychological value.

Thus, beside the *descriptive* documentary film is the *psychological* one.

I should like the making of documentary films of a psychological nature. I have a plan, which I shall now put forth, but the uncertainty of whether it could ever be financed has kept me from greatly elaborating my ideas, which require much preparation before they can be transferred to the screen. Even though it may not be mine, I am enthusiastic about the realization of any idea pertaining to this type of film.

I have here the plans, in embryonic state, of two themes which I should like to try on the screen. One is:*

*From a typescript in English. Written in 1938.*

*[The manuscript breaks off at this point.—Trans.]

# Pessimism

I have always been on the side of those who seek the truth, but I part ways with them when they think they have found it. They often become fanatics, which I detest, or if not, then ideologues: I am not an intellectual, and their speeches send me running. Like all speeches. For me, the best orator is the one who from the first phrase takes a pair of pistols from his pockets and fires on the audience.

I am a tranquil man who would have liked to be a writer or a painter. But I write with difficulty, with results that please me little. I am not very sensitive to color, and only figurative painting interests me, providing I like the scene it depicts. Nevertheless, in my youth I wrote a book that I never published composed of poems, essays, and stories. I called it *The Andalusian Dog*. But Dalí convinced me that the title was better suited to my first film, since there was nothing Andalusian in the film, nor did it have anything to do with a dog. We imagined that film together, when we were still friends. Dalí had dreamed about a pierced hand with ants crawling out of it, and I about a sliced eye. We went on that way, now taking images from our dreams, now looking for others, which we retained only if they didn't correspond to anything we already knew. Within eight days we had found enough material for a film, which I made with financial assistance from my mother.

Cinema had always been seductive for me, because it is a complete means of expression, alternately realistic and oneiric, narrative, absurd, or poetic. One day I saw Fritz Lang's *Der müde Tod*, and I think that the scene of the funeral procession that passes through a wall decided my profession. After *Un Chien andalou*, I was even more eager to keep making films. I returned to Paris, which fascinated me with its abundance of artistic life. I joined Breton, Eluard, and later the entire surrealist group, which was enraptured by my film, while Lorca hated it. I devised gags. I had some twenty of them ready but didn't have money for the film I wanted to make. With the help of friends, that film became *L'Age d'or*. Next, a wonderful book, written by a Frenchman who had spent part of his life in Las Hurdes, inspired *Land without Bread*.

I didn't make any more films for the next fifteen years. From Hollywood in the 1930s I received offers to produce films but not to direct them. Then I asked the surrealist group for permission to go to the U.S., which they granted. I wasn't very happy there, and when Dalí published a book in which he denounced me as an atheist, insinuating that I was a Communist (I never have been, nor an anarchist) and that I dreamed of nothing but revolt and disorder, I encountered so much trouble that I had to present my resignation. I fell out with Dalí and afterward went to live in Mexico. There I began to make movies again with *Gran Casino*, which I consider a bad film.

Every type of show has its own audience. The one that goes to the cinema is, in general, the least congenial of all. Waiting in line puts them in a bad mood; you'll never see in them the enthusiasm of a bullfight aficionado. At heart, it's a false audience that relates to no one, only to images. If these images are mundane, they put them to sleep; if they're nice, they distract them. The Americans, who have understood this perfectly, give priority to action. From my stay in the U.S., I still have a great admiration for American cinema, its actors, its sense of rhythm and action. Its filmmakers have handled with unique mastery a modern art that corresponds very well to the temperament of that people, perhaps because things technical play an essential role there. In any event, like them I have wanted to eliminate from my films the beautiful images in which European cinema, with the exception of Visconti, has often lost itself. I have felt tempted a few times: The opening of *Nazarín* could have been a superb image of Popocatepetl covered with snow, in a light worthy of the creation of the world. I shot that view. But I also wanted Nazarín to arrive on a road full of potholes, in a miserable and unattractive landscape. I chose the latter.

Consequently, in my films I grant particular importance to the action and strive constantly to create surprises. The point of departure is often a very simple idea: people who can't manage to eat (*The Discreet Charm of the Bourgeoisie*) or who are unable to leave a certain place (*The Exterminating Angel*). This idea is progressively developed until it becomes a very precise plot that guides me through the direction and editing. The editing, which puts together scenes shot randomly and brings unity to the film, is a matter of no more than two or three days. By contrast, the details of the shots are developed while filming, with the ongoing aim of breaking up the evolution of each scene, of creating ruptures. In *That Obscure Object of Desire*, at the moment in which Fernando Rey gives the mother money to meet with her daughter the next day, a rat falls from the ceiling. It's a rubber rat. I like surprises to provoke laughter, and I've made much use of objects, and of the fetishism they inspire, to create a comic effect. It's certainly true that fetishism bothers me in reality.

Filmmaking seems to me a transitory and threatened art. It is very closely bound up with technical developments. If in thirty or fifty years the screen no longer exists, if editing isn't necessary, cinema will have ceased to exist. It will have become something else. That's already almost the case when a film is shown on television: the smallness of the screen falsifies everything. What will remain, then, of my films? I don't think very highly at all of most of them. I have a certain fondness for only about ten, which isn't many in relation to all that I have made: *L'Age d'or*, above all; *Nazarín; Un Chien andalou; Simon of the Desert; Los Olvidados*, the preparation of which brought me in touch with juvenile delinquency and plunged me into the heart of Mexican misery; *Viridiana; Robinson Crusoe; The Criminal Life of Archibaldo de la Cruz; The Milky Way; The Discreet Charm of the Bourgeoisie . . .*

Those are the films that best express my vision of life. Surrealism made me understand that freedom and justice do not exist, but it also provided me with an ethic. An ethic of human solidarity, whose importance to me had been understood by Eluard and Breton when they humorously called me "the director of conscience" in their dedication to *The Immaculate Conception.* I illustrated this ethic in my own very particular way because I believe that my spirit is by nature destructive—and certainly of all of society. I have often returned to the subject of man struggling against a society that seeks to oppress and degrade him. Every individual seems to me worthy of interest, but when people congregate, their aggressiveness is set free and is converted into attack or flight, exercising violence or suffering. The history of heresies perfectly illustrates this, and that is why I have been so interested in them, as can be seen indirectly in many of my films, above all *The Milky Way.* It fascinates me to see how if a few men unite around a conviction, if they form a society founded on that conviction, it is enough for one of them to differ, even in the smallest way, for him to be treated as the vilest of enemies. A Protestant sect in the seventeenth century was persecuted simultaneously by Catholics and other Protestants because it maintained that the body of Christ was found in the host in the same way a rabbit is inside a pâté. To kill people for that seems to me an absurd monstrosity. I don't care for heretics, neither Luther nor Calvin. With them the mass was transformed into a boring lecture delivered in a mournful room by a man dressed in black. The Catholic Church at least had the merit of creating an architecture, a liturgy, a music that moves me. But I admire the man who remains true to his conscience, whatever it inspires in him. Although I have treated most of the protagonists in my films ironically, I never mocked Nazarín or Robinson Crusoe; I respected their purity. At bottom, I have always chosen man against men.

Today I have come to be much more pessimistic. I believe that our world is lost. It may be destroyed by the population explosion, technology, science, and information. I call these four horsemen of the apocalypse. I am frightened by modern science that leads us to the grave through nuclear war or genetic manipulations, if not through psychiatry, as in the Soviet Union. Europe must create a new civilization, but

I fear that science and the madness it can unleash won't leave time enough to do it.

If I had to make one last film, I would make it about the complicity of science and terrorism. Although I understand the motivations of terrorism, I totally disapprove of them. It solves nothing; it plays into the hands of the right and of repression. One of the themes of the film would be this: A band of international terrorists is preparing a severe attack in France, when the news arrives that an atomic bomb has been detonated over Jerusalem. A general mobilization is declared everywhere; world war is imminent. Then the leader of the group telephones the president of the Republic. He informs the French authorities of the exact location, in a barge near the Louvre, where they can recover the atomic bomb the terrorists have placed there before it explodes. His organization had decided to destroy the center of a civilization, but they renounced the crime because world war was about to break out, and the mission of terrorism had ended. Henceforth it is assumed by governments, which take up the task of destroying the world.

The glut of information has also brought about a serious deterioration in human consciousness today. If the pope dies, if a chief of state is assassinated, television is there. What good does it do one to be present everywhere? Today man can never be alone with himself, as he could in the Middle Ages.

The result of all this is that anguish is absolute and confusion total.

I knew an age in which the Right and the Left occupied well-defined positions. The struggle made some sense then. Now Soviet civilization seems to me just as tragic as the Western world. Is the only choice whether to take refuge in Moscow, which I hate, or in New York, which I don't like? I would choose New York, but with what sadness!

Sometimes I look for a glimmer of hope in this world of pessimism. I dream that science has become wiser, and the learned have become conscious of their responsibility.

In the film I'm thinking about, I would have liked to shoot in the hall of the Reichstag a meeting of fifteen Nobel prize–winning scientists recommending that atomic bombs be placed at the bottom of all oil wells. Science would then cure us of that which feeds our madness. But I rather think that in the end we'll be borne off by the worst, because since *Un Chien andalou* the world has advanced toward the absurd.

I am the only one who hasn't changed. I remain Catholic and atheist, thank God.

*From the Spanish. Written in 1980.*

# Afterword

Juan Luis Buñuel and Rafael Buñuel

"A desperate call for murder": that was the meaning of *L'Age d'or*. And now, as time goes by, Luis Buñuel's image has softened; people have begun to see him as a mythological, museum-bound figure. Before, when one of his films came out, crowds would tear up the theater; liberal politicians would censor his works or demand that he be expelled from the country he was living in. That's what his films and writings were all about. To provoke, to shock, to destroy a society that he found corrupt and idiotic, to ridicule a religion that had oppressed millions of people, and continues to do so. "The search for Truth is wonderful. Beware of the person who then claims to have found that Truth."

Some towns in Spain that are governed by right-wing politicians have named streets after him. Don't they know what he thought of them? How he and his comrades fought against them during the Civil War, against their mentality. He has become their hero; his name brings the tourists in . . .

Now many of his books and belongings have been put into museums. Yet the last script he wrote was about a group of young terrorists who wanted to bomb the Louvre in Paris. In the end they didn't do it. Disillusioned by today's society, they came to the conclusion that humanity didn't need any help to destroy itself.

Buñuel must not be remembered as a politically correct individual. He was a kind man—but also a violent one, vengeful against a bourgeois social system that has always suppressed the emotions of freedom and love in humanity.

Designer:       Nola Burger
Compositor:     G & S Typesetters, Inc.
Text:           10/15 Janson
Display:        Franklin Gothic Book and Demi
Printer/binder: Bookcrafters